Wisdom ~ Compassion ~ Serenity

First Steps on the Buddhist Path

M. Sekiyo Sullivan

DEDICATION

To Michelle.

CONTENTS

ACKNOWLEDGMENTS

This is not "my" book. This book is just my attempt to connect readers with the Buddha, Dharma and Sangha. I could not possibly have completed this work without a good deal of help and support.

First, I have had the incredibly good fortune of being able to know and learn from two very special people, Than Chaokhun Sunan Phra Vijitrdhammapani, the abbot of Wat Florida Dhammaram, and Rev. Koyo S. Kubose, the spiritual and administrative head of Bright Dawn Center for Oneness Buddhism.

I list them in order of appearance in my life: I studied Theravada Buddhism and meditation with Than Chaokhun beginning in 2005, ordained for an all-too-short monastic retreat at Wat Florida and visited Thailand with him. I spent two years in the Bright Dawn program learning more than I imagined possible from Rev. Kubose about day-to-day dharma and the work of being a Sensei.

There is no way to quantify the importance of the roles they have played in my spiritual growth and my development as a dharma teacher. Much of this book's content developed from notes I took during dharma talks at Wat Florida Dhammaram and reports I wrote while studying with Bright Dawn, so in a very real sense, this work owes as much to Than Chaokhun and Rev. Kubose as to me.

There are many other teachers, famous and not-so-famous, whose work has inspired and informed me, and I thank them for their efforts.

I also want to thank supporters like Sooz Renyo, Jim and Greg, whose confidence in me has been so energizing, the members of Volusia Buddhist Fellowship, the congregation at All Souls Unitarian in Palatka, inmates at Tomoka Correctional Institution and many others who have done me the honor of listening to me talk about the dharma. If I have attained any competence as a teacher, it is because I have had great students.

I bow deeply to my wife, Michelle, whose love and encouragement has been such a blessing; to my mom, who has given so much of her energy and resources to my spiritual journey; and to my son, who has stood beside me so often through this process.

FORWARD
By Rev. Koyo S. Kubose

Morris Sekiyo Sullivan has written a book that gives a great introduction to understanding the basics of the Buddhist tradition. What he expresses on such topics as faith, the Paramitas, the Four Noble Truths, the Four Seals of the Dharma—and how these topics are related to Wisdom, Compassion, and Serenity—is informative to all Buddhists, regardless of their backgrounds.

Sullivan's combination of personal anecdotes and sutra quotations is particularly effective in communicating the Dharma teachings. With the simple clarity that shows his sincerity, Sullivan provides solid grounding to help others walk the Buddhist path.

As D.T. Suzuki has stated, "There are three qualities necessary to successfully walk the Buddhist path. The first is sincerity; the second is sincerity; and the third is sincerity." I have witnessed such sincerity as Sekiyo Sullivan progressed through our Bright Dawn Center's Lay Ministry Program and in his subsequent Dharma work.

The karmic effects of this sincerity are like Dharma seeds sown along the path of Sullivan's own spiritual journey. May his sharing through this book to a wider Sangha provide blossoms ranging from fine roses to hardy wildflowers. How Buddhaful!

INTRODUCTION

One Sunday morning, I sat in the front row of a Unitarian congregation in a small Central Florida town where I had been invited to give the sermon. As I listened to the service leader introduce me, I realized that my two-paragraph bio included bits and pieces of several languages over which she stumbled.

I have a Japanese dharma name (Sekiyo) and title (Sensei), because my ministerial tradition is based on Japanese Mahayana Buddhism. "Mahayana" is Sanskrit, but I was ordained in a Theravada (that's Pali) order at Wat Florida Dhammaram (Thai/Southeast Asian) in Kissimmee, Florida. Had I provided a more thorough bio, I could have tossed in a little Vietnamese and Tibetan, too, but I was glad I hadn't.

The poor woman apologized as I approached the podium. "I know I mispronounced a lot," she said.

"I thought you did pretty well," I answered. "Most people get 'Kissimmee' wrong."

That exchange got a nice laugh and broke the ice, but it also points out one of the challenges Americans have when they approach Buddhism: The teachings have passed through so many cultures on their way to us that even the basics can seem confusing due to language and cultural variations.

There are two main collections of early Buddhist teachings, one in Pali and another in Sanskrit. While many important words are similar, they're not identical—the Sanskrit *karma* is *kamma* in Pali, for example.

Eventually, Western Buddhism will probably settle on a language of its own. In the meantime, however, I had to decide what I thought made sense in the context of my practice and for the people I hope will read this book. In the case of words that have largely been absorbed into English, like karma, dharma and nirvana, I went with the familiar Sanskrit forms except where they appear in the titles of sutras from the Pali canon; I kept the Pali in order to make the sutras easier to find online.

The process gets a little trickier with words like *metta* (Pali) and *maitri* (Sanskrit). Those familiar with Insight/Vipassana meditation will have worked with metta while others who have done similar Tibetan practices will know the Sanskrit version. Since the core of my own meditation practice has come from the Theravada Vipassana tradition, I elected to use the Pali terms.

On the same subject, metta and some other Pali words have no truly accurate equivalents in English. Rather than use inadequate translations, I opted to define or explain those terms on first reference and then simply use the Pali form thereafter.

Unless otherwise noted, sutras cited come from the Pali canon. Most have been excerpted and adapted for reasons of space, form and, where necessary, to add meaning that was removed from the context during the excerpting process.

In the coming chapters, I will try to present an approach to the Buddhist path I feel can give a newcomer a start toward a life of practice, and I will try to keep the presentation relatively free from sectarian concerns. It is impossible to present every possible point of view, so it is inevitable that I will leave out things that others will find important.

Also, many of the teachings work on different levels and have different uses. I have tried to avoid a lot of analysis and to stick with the approach to each teaching that seems most practical on a day-to-day basis for most people looking for an approach to the dharma, based on my experience.

It is common in some Buddhist traditions when writing a book about the dharma to apologize for any errors or omissions the author makes. Having worked with this material for some time, I understand why: Inevitably, the writer must present a point of view by using words with inherent shortcomings and then hope the meaning is conveyed adequately.

Please accept my apology for any misrepresentations, omissions or oversights that occurred here due to my lack of skill, understanding or spiritual realization.

May all beings always live happily,
Free from animosity.
May all share in the blessings
That spring from the good we have done.

ABOUT BUDDHISM

Every spring, my front yard blooms with spiderwort. Native plant enthusiasts might argue otherwise, but spiderwort is pretty much a weed. The flowers are pretty, though—the blooms range from electric blue to violet with bright yellow anthers—and they attract butterflies and fat black-and-yellow bumblebees. I have tried to cultivate spiderwort in flowerbeds alongside more domesticated flowers. I have tried transplanting them and have even bought potted ones at the annual Native Plant Society sale. However, spiderwort seems determined to grow everywhere except where I want it.

I once discussed spiderwort with the pastor of a nearby historic Baptist church. I admitted a little sheepishly that I put off the first spring mowing of my lawn as long as possible so I could enjoy the blooms. He admitted he did the same thing. We agreed they are at least a good excuse to avoid mowing the lawn.

Like spiderwort, the dharma doesn't always show itself where you want or expect to find it. You might sit down on your meditation cushion to "listen" for a teaching to arise from your peaceful heart and find nothing but noise. You might travel to a famous dharma center for a retreat with a legendary teacher and learn next to nothing. But then there you are on the treadmill at the gym, in the checkout line at the grocery store or mowing your front yard, and you come face to face with Universal Truth.

I have been interested in Buddhism much of my life, but my practice was sporadic and I really didn't call myself "a Buddhist" until my wife and I began sitting with a fledgling meditation group, which reawakened a meditation practice that had lain dormant for a while. I enjoyed meditating and reading about the teachings of the Buddha, but I can't say I was getting a lot out of it at until one morning when I took our then-puppy, Faust, out for a walk.

My neighborhood goes from suburban to rural a few blocks west of my house. Just past the point where the sidewalk ends and cow pastures begin, the dog and I have to walk in the road along a stretch where Spanish bayonets grow right next to the pavement. There's usually not much traffic in the morning, so drivers will move over to give us room to walk without getting skewered by their dagger-like leaves.

That morning, as Faust and I reached the point where the growth was at its thickest, a pickup came over a hill toward us. I expected the driver to drift toward his left; there was no other traffic, so he could easily do that. He came closer and closer, however, still hugging the shoulder until the last minute when I yanked on the leash and pulled Faust into the Spanish bayonet with me.

I stared dumbfounded at the driver as he passed. I could see him gripping his wheel, scowling as he passed, as if to say we should stay the heck out of his street! I was so angry! I couldn't believe the lack of consideration, the outright meanness of this jackass, this stupid old jerk, this—

...and as I turned to watch him drive away, I saw the sun over the crest of the next hill, its bright morning rays shining right into my eyes so that I could see neither the truck nor anything else on the road. This poor guy I had deemed a scowling, inconsiderate jackass had been blinded by the sun that was just peering over the horizon. He hadn't even seen us as he squinted into the light and tried to keep his vehicle on the road.

I felt deflated. I had come face-to-face with my anger and with the realization that my mental fabrications about the driver of the pickup had flown so far off the mark. I felt slightly nauseous, but at the same time, the true importance of my Buddhist practice dawned on me.

I once heard a weed defined as "a plant for which no one has yet discovered a use." Of course, we shouldn't cultivate anger—we'd better yank it up by the roots and cultivate more skillful emotional states. But once in a while, perhaps even anger can point us toward important knowledge about our true nature.

A few springs later, as I prepared to go to California for induction as a Bright Dawn Center of Oneness Buddhism sensei, I noticed the spiderwort in my yard was especially prolific. For whatever reason, by the time the grass had started looking shaggy, the patches of spiderwort had gotten thicker than ever, the plants taller than I remembered them being in the past.

I stood in my front yard admiring the spiderwort and thinking I really needed to mow the lawn. It dawned on me that maybe, instead of flowers belonging where the gardener puts the flowerbeds, the flowerbeds belong where the flowers grow. I got the lawnmower out of the shed and carefully began mowing around my new spiderwort beds.

A book about the dharma is not the dharma. In a book, sentences describing the dharma are put into "order," much like the flowerbeds of a carefully designed garden, where each plant is placed where it will look its best. If the book is well planned and well written, the topics fall into an order that showcases each appropriately relative to the others. The dharma, however, is much more willfully organic—like spiderwort, it grows where it grows. And like spiderwort, it lets the viewer take responsibility for its recognition and appreciation.

This book is intended to give the reader a basis to begin practicing Buddhism, and I have tried to present that in an orderly fashion. Once outside these pages, however, the reader shouldn't expect to encounter the dharma in an orderly fashion. Reading about the dharma may be a chapter-by-chapter proposition, but realizing the dharma happens moment by moment.

As you read this book, I encourage you to meditate on what you read, examine what you read and analyze what you read. But I also encourage you to put down the book once in a while and see how the dharma makes itself known in your life and to nourish it, wherever it decides to grow.

The Origins of Buddhism

Siddhartha Gautama, the man we call "the Buddha," was born almost 2,600 years ago in an Asian state then known as Sakka, which lay in the foothills of the Himalayas in present-day Nepal. The religious life of the region was fairly diverse at the time. Most people in India observed Brahmanism, the historical precursor to contemporary Hinduism. There were also ascetics who practiced various forms of yoga and followers of Jainism, an ancient religion that emphasizes nonviolence and non-materialism.

Sakka was ruled by Suddhodana, who lived in the capital city of Kapilavastu with his queen, Mahamaya Devi. It was customary in those days for a woman to travel to her parents home to give birth, so one morning, when Queen Mahamaya was ready to bear her first child, she left the palace bound for her parents' home. Around noon, she and her retinue stopped at a grove in Lumbini and rested in the shade of a Sala tree, where she suddenly went into labor. While standing up grasping a branch of the tree, Mahamaya delivered an infant son.

Five days later, King Suddhodana arranged a naming ceremony for the child he would call Siddhartha, which means "fulfilling a wish." The king had asked 108 distinguished holy men to come bless the infant, and each sage made predictions about the boy's future. With one exception, each said Siddhartha would either become a great king who would unite all of India or a great religious leader. The one standout, Kondañña, said the infant would grow up to be the greatest religious leader the world had seen—one who would liberate humanity.

Queen Mahamaya was weakened by Siddhartha's delivery and never recovered her strength. She died a few days after the ceremony, and Suddhodana brought her sister, princess Mahapajapati, to the palace to care for his son.

Suddhodana wanted his son to become a king, not a sage. He tried to give Siddhartha every comfort secular life could provide, making sure the young prince had the best food, clothing and material pleasures available. He also hired the best teacher available at the time to educate Siddhartha in everything necessary to run a kingdom, including martial arts and administrative skills.

An episode from the prince's early life foreshadows what is to come, however. Each spring, a plowing festival was held to commemorate the end of winter and the beginning of the growing season. King Suddhodana would open each festival by ceremonially breaking the ground with a bejeweled plow, and then everyone would dance and celebrate.

One year, the king had Siddhartha's attendants bring him to the festival, and they set the young boy in the shade of a tree to watch the plowing. As the king walked behind the plow, Siddhartha noticed that while the people attending the festival seemed to be having a great time, the king's oxen did not seem so happy—they struggled as they strained to pull the blade through the hard ground. He also saw that birds eagerly followed the plow to feast on the worms and insects suddenly made vulnerable as the ground was opened.

As young as he was, Siddhartha came to the painful realization about suffering. There, sitting in the shade and watching this dance of life and death, the boy was moved by a great surge of compassion and suddenly and spontaneously entered a state of jhana, meditative absorption, his sadness replaced by waves of bliss and then equanimity.

How could viewing the death of insects and worms lead to a blissful mental state? Siddhartha must have realized in his meditation that if there was suffering, there was an end of suffering, thus this plowing ceremony was a harbinger of the liberation to come. Later, many Buddhist scriptures would use plowing as a metaphor for the dharma, like this verse from the Kasi Bharadvaja Sutta:

Faith is my seed, practice my rain, discernment my yoke and plow,
  And persistence my beast of burden.
Having plowed this plowing, one is unyoked from suffering—
  The fruit it yields is deathlessness!

Siddhartha was an excellent student, and by age 15 he had mastered everything his teacher could offer. When he was 16 years old, his father arranged his marriage to Bimba Yasodhara, a princess from Devadaha. Still determined to keep Siddhartha's mind from religion, he gave the couple three palaces, one for each season, and made sure his son, the heir to the leadership of Kapilavastu, had every possible entertainment available to him.

When Siddhartha was 29 years old, Yasodhara became pregnant. By then, the prince had developed a curiosity about the world outside the walls of his palaces and begun riding through the city he would one day rule accompanied by his attendant, Channa.

The king had instructed his son's servants that whenever Siddhartha prepared to leave the palace, they must make sure he would see nothing unpleasant. Streets were to be cleaned and homes decorated before the prince passed, and only healthy, happy people were allowed to be outdoors at the time.

Despite their efforts, however, a decrepit elderly man appeared in the street one day when Siddhartha and Channa rode through the city. Siddhartha was shocked at the sight of a gray-haired, wrinkled, half-blind creature with bent spine and toothless mouth.

"What is that?" he anxiously asked Channa. He didn't even recognize the being he saw as human.

"It's a man," Channa replied. "He's an old man. He wasn't born like this—he was once straight and strong, with clear eyes and black hair, like you. This is what age does to all people, if they live long enough."

Siddhartha was stunned. He asked to be taken home, where he spent the rest of the day and night thinking about this disturbing revelation. In a few days, however, he prepared to leave the palace again. This time, he ordered his servants not to make any special arrangements; he wanted to see the city in its natural state.

He spotted another strange sight during this ride—a man moaning in agony, struggling for breath, his body wracked by disease.

"Why is that man like this?" Siddhartha asked Channa as he dismounted to try to help the man.

"His body is poisoned by disease," said Channa, warning the prince to keep his distance. All humans were subject to illnesses like this, he explained.

About that time, a group of people turned down the street, weeping and carrying a motionless, thin and wasted man stretched out on a board. They laid the man atop a pile of wood, which they began to light on fire.

"Why doesn't he run away?" Siddhartha wondered.

"He has died," Channa said. "His feet can't run; his eyes can't see; he feels nothing; he knows nothing. He doesn't even know he's dead."

Death was another unknown—the prince had been insulated from seeing or hearing about it. Channa explained, to Siddhartha's dismay, that all beings eventually enter this state. Siddhartha's father, stepmother, and even Siddhartha himself would eventually die.

The prince returned home in silence. He must have noticed signs of aging had begun to appear on his father's face. His stepmother would soon grow old. His wife, his trusted attendants, and even Siddhartha himself might become ill, and all would eventually lie in the flames of the funeral pyre. Consumed with such thoughts, Siddhartha vowed to study the problem, to look for a way he and his loved ones might escape the powerful grip of old age, disease and death.

A few days later, Siddhartha visited the royal gardens where he saw another unexpected sight—a man dressed in orange robes, his face bathed in a light of calm and serenity. Channa explained the orange-robed stranger was a *bikkhu*, a man who had left the world to look for a remedy for its sufferings and sorrows. Siddhartha was thrilled to learn there were others who sought a way to transcend aging, illness and death.

When he returned to the palace, however, he was greeted with important news: Yasodhara had born him a son. To the surprise of his attendants, Siddhartha was not happy. He decided to name his son Rahula—"noose" or "fetter"—because his birth bound him more tightly to the world of sorrow and suffering.

Siddhartha spent the rest of the day deep in thought. That evening, he went to see his wife, who lay sleeping with Rahula. Siddhartha was deeply disheartened by the idea that he, his wife, son and everyone else he held dear would suffer illness, old age and death. He had decided to look for the bikkhu and to follow in the search for liberation. He could not bear to wake his wife; he knew if he looked into her eyes and held his son, he would never leave.

Siddhartha crept out quietly and asked Channa to saddle his favorite horse. They rode together out of the city until dawn, when they reached the river that bordered Sakka on the south. On the bank of the river, the prince took out his sword and cut the knot that bound the long hair on top of his head. He handed the knot of hair to Channa with instructions to carry it to his wife, and then removed his fine clothes to don simple robes. Channa rode back toward the palace, and Siddhartha walked ahead alone.

Many people are shocked when they hear this story of Siddhartha abandoning his family to go off in self-pursuit. Bear in mind, however, that when Siddhartha lived, marriages were more a matter of business than romance and men of his status were likely to go away to war or on business for long periods. That doesn't mean he had no responsibility for his wife and child, of course, but his wife and son held an important place in the king's domain and would be cared for.

We might also imagine that the birth of his son was a pivotal incident in

Siddhartha's path. Seeing his heir come into the world already subject to all of life's stress and suffering may well have provided the final motivation that encouraged him to give up his comfortable secular life in favor of the hardships of the spiritual life. As he explained in the Ariyapariyesana Sutta:

Being subject to birth, I sought what was also subject to birth. Being subject to aging, to illness, to death and sorrow, I sought happiness in things that were subject to aging, illness, death and sorrow. Finally the thought occurred to me, 'What if I sought that which is not subject to birth—the deathless?' Thus, while still enjoying the blessings of youth, I shaved off my hair, donned the ochre robe and went forth into homelessness.

Siddhartha went to Magadha, where he asked for instruction from two yogis, Alara and Addaka. Each taught him his own style of meditation, and Siddhartha very quickly mastered every practice the yogis could teach him. However, he soon realized those practices would not take him to his goal.

He next took up asceticism. Siddhartha excelled at extreme self-mortification such as going without sleep and living on almost no food or drink. Five of the Brahmins who had attended his naming ceremony soon joined him. Certain that Siddhartha would live up to their prediction that he would be a great religious leader, they had decided to practice alongside him, hoping that when he attained the dharma of deliverance they would share in his realization.

Siddhartha took asceticism to its limits, fasting and struggling until he became so emaciated his spine stood out like a strand of beads and his facial features so shrunken he looked like a skull. One day, thoroughly exhausted, he fell to the ground, where he might have died if a goatherd had not seen him there and fed him some milk.

As the milk soaked into his starving tissues and Siddhartha's strength began to recover, he realized six years of practice had led nowhere. This extreme asceticism was not the way to liberation, after all, and he determined to begin taking care of his body so he would have the strength to continue his search.

Soon afterward, a young woman came to his hermitage to offer him a bowl of rice cooked in rich milk, which he accepted. When his five companions saw Siddhartha had begun to eat good food again, they believed he had given up his practice and gone back to a life of ease. Disappointed, they left him there alone and went to the Deer Park, a refuge in Sarnath near Varanasi.

His companions were mistaken, however. Siddhartha was more determined than ever to reach his goal of complete liberation, and he realized he was on the brink of an important realization. He sat at the base of a tree near the Neranjara river, determined to stay there until he reached enlightenment.

"My blood may dry up, my bones may crumble to dust," he vowed. "But I will not rise until I have found the way out of samsara—the cycle of impermanence and dissatisfaction—and found the way to the deathless state of Nirvana."

He meditated for several days and nights, wrestling with Mara, the troubles and temptations that plagued his mind. At last, during the final hours of the seventh night, Siddhartha reached down to touch the ground on which he sat, calling the earth to witness his liberation. He had realized the truth of arising and cessation:

When this is, that is.
From the arising of this comes the arising of that.
When this isn't, that isn't.
From the cessation of this comes the cessation of that.

As this grows clear
Ardent, absorbed, he stands —
Routing the dark troops of Mara,
Like the sun that chases darkness
from the sky.

The Middle Way

I was practicing tai chi in the park one Sunday morning, and a couple of teenagers stopped to watch and chat. They eventually had to leave for church, but before they left, one mentioned he was having trouble "relating to" religion. He was struggling to figure out where it fit into his life and how to approach it.

Religious practice is like a wellness program for the spirit, I explained. If you have a heart attack, you go to the cardiologist. Perhaps you go on medication, and maybe you even get surgery. But you don't have to wait until you have heart disease to start taking care of your heart. If you can build a good foundation for wellness, maybe you won't ever have a heart attack.

Similarly, if you take good care of your spiritual health, you can save yourself a lot of crises—a lot of trouble—later down the line. So maybe he could see religious practice as something like a wellness program for the *other* heart—not the physical organ that pumps blood, but that part of the mind where spirituality resides.

One way or another, every religious practice could be considered an attempt to alleviate, eliminate or otherwise address human suffering. When the Buddha was enlightened, he realized a path of practice that an ordinary human being could follow and thus transcend suffering. So in his time, he was sometimes referred to as the "supreme physician."

After his awakening, Siddhartha—now the Buddha—spent seven weeks examining his own mind to determine if his enlightenment was complete and authentic. It occurred to him that the meaning of his dharma would be difficult for people to grasp. Thinking few people could understand what he had to say, he considered not teaching.

Eventually, however, he realized different beings have different capacities to hear and understand. "In a pond, some lotuses might flourish while immersed in the water, without ever rising up from the depths," he thought. "Some might stand at even level with the surface. Others might rise from the water and stand high above it."

Likewise, some beings would be hard to teach while others could easily learn. Moved by compassion, he set out to share his dharma. The Buddha recalled the five ascetics who had abandoned him after he began to take meals again and realized they would probably understand his teaching. He went to look for them and caught up with them at the Deer Park. At first, his former companions refused to welcome him, but he finally convinced them he had found what they had all sought. He spent the night at the preserve and gave his first sermon the following day.

This sermon, known in the Pali Canon as the *Dhammacakkappavattana Sutta*, or the Sutra Setting the Wheel of Dharma in Motion, is probably the best known of the Buddha's teachings. It contains the foundation for Buddhist practice, the Four Noble Truths and the Eightfold Path.

When he gave that first sermon, the Buddha laid out his Middle Way to spiritual health beginning with the Four Noble Truths: There is suffering; suffering has a cause; if the cause is correctly understood suffering can be transcended; and the Noble Eightfold Path is the way to that transcendence.

The First Noble Truth defined the problem: "There is suffering." Actually, the term used is *dukkha*, which includes a lot of different forms and levels of stress and dissatisfaction. Dukkha includes the physical suffering of birth, aging, illness and death. It also includes the more relative, psychological kinds of suffering—union with things we don't like, separation from those we do like, not attaining what we desire, and the instability of physical and mental circumstances.

In the Second Noble Truth, the Buddha pointed out something psychologists would revisit 2,500 years later: Suffering is for the most part caused not by external factors but by mental processes like ignorance, craving and irrationalities that cling to our consciousness and keep us trapped in the cycle of suffering.

The causes of suffering have been further categorized as the six fundamental obstructions, which include the three poisons—greed, anger and ignorance—along with pride, doubt and wrong views. The Third Noble Truth states that if we can transcend the causes of suffering, we can transcend the suffering. And the Fourth Noble Truth lays out the Noble Eightfold Path to that transcendence.

We will explore the eightfold path in more depth later, but it can help to understand the path if we view it as a three-fold training in wisdom, ethics and concentration. Just as factors like proper nutrition, a supportive social network and regular exercise can help us stay in good physical health, the threefold training can help us stay spiritually healthy.

Thus a Buddhist can practice seeing situations and circumstances as they are, behaving skillfully so as to minimize suffering for oneself and others, and identifying and eliminating harmful mental states while developing and maintaining helpful mental states. This practice can keep our spiritual heartbeat strong.

There are two extremes not to be indulged in by one who has gone forth—that which is devoted to sensual pleasure, and that which is devoted to self-affliction. Avoiding both extremes, the middle way leads to serenity, to knowledge, to awakening, to freedom. What is the middle way? Precisely this Noble Eightfold Path: Right View, Right Resolve, Right Speech, Right Action, Right Livelihood, Right Effort, Right Mindfulness and Right Concentration. This is the middle way that leads to serenity, to knowledge, to awakening, to freedom.[1]

After hearing the Buddha's sermon on the Four Noble Truths, the Dharma Eye—the "spotless, immaculate vision of the dharma," arose in the ascetic Kondañña. He immediately asked the Buddha to ordain him and thus became the first of the Buddha's monks. Within a few days, each of the remaining four was admitted into the Buddha's new monastic order.

By now, each monk understood the truth of dukkha, its origin and the path to its end. Each understood the nature of impermanence: All that arises is subject to cessation. The Buddha had also explained that sentient beings are made up of form—a physical body made from various elements and fueled by combustion—along with the formless conditions of feeling, perception, volition and consciousness.

The Buddha and his fledgling monastic order stayed at the Deer Park during the rainy season. One night, a wealthy young man named Yasa awoke in the early morning hours. In the dim light, he could see his concubines sleeping. He noticed that, in their careless and immodest sleeping poses, they looked more like corpses than beautiful women. Suddenly filled with disgust, Yasa went outside for a walk.

---

[1] Dhammacakkappavattana Sutta

Lost in thought about his sudden realization that his home and life were loathsome, he continued walking until he encountered the Buddha, who was doing walking meditation in the early morning light. The Buddha heard him complaining about the dolefulness of his existence and began to teach him about the Themes of Progressive Importance, beginning with generosity and virtue and ending with the Four Noble Truths. By the end of their talk, Yasa had become a disciple.

By then, the young man's family had discovered his absence and organized to go look for him. His father arrived at the Deer Park, and seeing Yasa's sandals began to question the Buddha about his son's whereabouts. When the Buddha finished telling the elderly man that his son had become a monk and explaining his teachings, Yasa's father also ordained.

Within a few days, several of Yasa's friends, his mother and his former wife had heard the dharma and had become monks or lay supporters. The Buddha soon had 60 monks staying with him.

When the rainy season ended, the Buddha called his monks together. He knew there was much suffering in the world, and he realized these *arahants*—fully enlightened followers—could help many people. He explained that as they had been freed from the bonds that chained them to dukkha, each should go out and teach his dharma to as many people as possible. The Buddha himself would go back toward Gaya to teach.

The Buddha didn't always teach as a formal ritual, but often found opportunities to turn relatively mundane situations into teachings. While on his way to Gaya, he gave one of those teachings to a group of 30 young men.

The men had gone on into the woods on an outing with their wives. One of the men was unmarried, however, and had brought a prostitute along. After they picnicked, everyone took a nap except for the prostitute, who made off with their valuables. When they awoke to discover the theft, the men set off in pursuit. They came across the Buddha meditating peacefully under a tree and asked if he had seen the woman.

"Which do you think is more important," the Buddha wondered. "To seek that woman, or to seek yourselves?"

The men were intrigued. They agreed it was better to seek themselves and abandoned their pursuit of the woman to hear the Buddha's teachings. All became followers.

The Buddha was a very good teacher, not so much because he could explain his dharma in intricate detail or in flowery language but because he could speak to each person in a way he or she would best understand his message. That required him to be sensitive to the student so that he could find the perfect note that would resonate with the individual.

As with Yasa, the Buddha started out by teaching the men about the

Themes of Progressive Importance. The first of those factors is *dana*—generosity. So in a sense, he began by telling these people who were pursuing a thief that to find themselves, they had to first let go of exactly that which they were pursuing.

Later that same day, the Buddha came to the shore of the river Neranjara, where 1,000 hermits lived. These hermits were students of three brothers, Uruvela, Nadi and Gaya, who were regarded as holy men by the local laity. When he arrived, the Buddha went to Uruvela and asked to spend the night at the hermitage. Uruvela agreed and directed him to spend the night in a shed which he knew sheltered venomous snakes. In the middle of the night, several of the hermits went to the shed, expecting to find the Buddha dead; instead, they found him silently doing walking meditation untroubled by the snakes.

By the time he left the hermitage, the Buddha had ordained all 1,000 of the hermits. Each became an arahant after hearing the Buddha deliver the Fire Sermon, in which he explained the different ways suffering resides in the mind and how it can be extinguished.

Some time later, the Buddha led the hermits to Rajgir. On the full moon day of the Magha lunar month, the Buddha went to the nearby Bamboo Grove to find all 1,000 of the hermits and another 250 mendicants assembled there. All 1,250 monks had been ordained by the Buddha himself, all were arahants, and all had arrived unbidden. The Buddha took this opportunity to deliver a special sermon which summarized his doctrine:

Patience and forgiveness is the highest austerity
  And liberation is foremost.
He is no monk who injures another;
  Nor is he a monk who mistreats another.
The non-doing of any evil,
  The performance of what's good,
To cleanse one's mind—
  This is the Buddha's teaching.
Not disparaging, not injuring,
  Restrained in conduct,
Observing moderation in food,
  Abiding in seclusion,
Committed to the highest states of mind:
  This is the Buddha's teaching.[2]

With more than 1,000 fully enlightened monks and numerous lay supporters, the Buddha's dharma was spreading quickly. In the second year

---

[2] Ovada-patimokkha Gatha

after his enlightenment, the Buddha returned to his hometown. Accompanied by a number of monks, he arrived back at Kapilavastu, where he gave teachings to his father and relatives.

His son, Rahula, asked him for ordination and became the first novice to become an arahant. Rahula's mother, Yasodhara, also eventually became an arahant. The Buddha's foster mother, Mahapajapati Gotami, established the order of *bhikkhunis* (female monks) and became the first female arahant.

After the rainy season ended that first year after he set the wheel of dharma in motion, the Buddha traveled toward Savatthi, where a wealthy man called Anathapindika lived. Anathapindika was renowned for being charitable toward the indigent, and when he heard of the Buddha's arrival, he arranged a welcoming ceremony and purchased a plot of heavily wooded land from a prince named Jeta.

Anathapindika paid an enormous amount of money for the grove, where he set about building housing for the Buddha and other monks. The Buddha would spend many rainy seasons at this first monastery, but he spent the rest of his remaining years wandering through India, teaching anyone who sought his message. He ordained thousands of monks and converted countless laypersons.

During the 45th year after his enlightenment, the Buddha became ill while spending the rains period at a village in Vesali. The illness continued to plague him for several months. When the Buddha realized that he would pass away soon, he took pains to make sure his monks' educations were complete.

Finally, accompanied by his cousin Ananda, who had been his attendant for 24 years, the Buddha gradually made his way toward Kushinagar, where he decided to rest in a grove of Sala trees. There, on the full moon day of the Vesak month, the first full moon in May, he had Ananda make his bed. The Buddha meditated, gave instructions to his monks, and ordained one final monk—a man named Subhadda, who came to visit him that night. The Buddha asked the monks who assembled in his presence if there were any questions remaining unanswered. Finally, he gave his final instruction:

"I remind you, monks: All conditioned things are subject to decline and decay. Be heedful!" With those words, he closed his eyes and entered meditative absorption. He passed away during the night.

After his funeral, the monks assembled and appointed a successor to head the sangha. Their new leader, Ven. Mahakassapa, proposed the order should begin collecting and classifying the teachings. The monks selected Ananda and 499 arahants to begin the process.

Ananda, by the way, was not yet enlightened. However, he had an excellent memory and had been the Buddha's main attendant for so long that he knew more of the teachings than anyone else. The other monks encouraged him to practice hard and to try to become an arahant before they assembled for the rainy season. On the first day of the assembly, Ananda, exhausted from his practices, started to lie down for a rest. Before his head touched the floor, he was suddenly enlightened. Thus the first assembly was attended by 500 arahants.

This first conference lasted seven months. There were two similar sessions during the next 224 years. The Buddha's teachings were initially preserved orally but were eventually written in Pali and Sanskrit, collected in the *Tipitaka*—the Three Baskets of teachings. The *Sutta Pitika* includes the collected discourses given by the Buddha and some of his closest disciples, the *Vinaya Pitika* includes the monastic rules and regulations and the *Abhidhamma Pitika* includes commentaries and systematizations of the dharma.

Today, Buddhism consists of three main branches: Theravada Buddhism from southeast Asia; Mahayana traditions from Japan, China, Korea and elsewhere; and Vajrayana schools from Tibet. Theravada traditions still mainly use the Pali Canon, while Mahayana and Vajrayana Buddhists refer to the Sanskrit texts.

If there was once a unified *dhamma-vinaya* (doctrine and discipline), regional differences like climate, culture and geography has since caused Buddhist lineages to evolve in different directions, and schisms had formed in the sangha as early as the 3rd Century BC.

The first of these schisms came between the southern and northern Buddhists and began when a group of reformers, the Mahasangika order, reacted to what they saw as an undue concern with strict, literal interpretation of the sutras and dogmatic adherence to tradition. The Mahasangikas believed interpretations of the dharma based on deeper meanings would be truer to the Buddha's original intentions.

Much of Buddhist discipline had by that time become very scholastic in its orientation with an emphasis on Abhidhamma study and philosophy. The reformers felt the Abhidhammists gave all the teachings the same level of importance and got wrapped up in minutiae rather than emphasizing the teachings that were genuinely profound.

The reform movement also felt the bodhisattva ideal—the idea that one practiced not for one's own benefit, but for the sake of others—had been overlooked and that too much emphasis was placed on monasticism. As a result, Mahayana Buddhism turned away from the arahant ideal, preferring to emphasize the salvation of laypersons and common people through relatively simple practices.

The disputes led to reflection and reform on both sides, and both interpretations of the dharma continued to survive and spread. The successful spread of Mahayana Buddhism came in part due the work of Nagarjuna, who set forth explanations of emptiness and anatta (not-self) sometime between 150 and 250 A.D. While he was admired by both sides, his works became a cornerstone of Mahayana thought. The foundation of Mahayana philosophy was more or less complete by 300 A.D.

Eventually, most of the southern Buddhist sects died off. Only Theravada (Way of the Elders) survived and became the dominant religion of Sri Lanka, Thailand and elsewhere in Southeast Asia.

During the 7th and 8th centuries, Tantric sects began to appear in India. The Vajrayana Buddhists taught that practitioners could achieve enlightenment with the aid of mandalas, mantras and deity worship, which symbolically embodied complex teachings. Vajrayana flourished in India for some time, but the prosperous Buddhist monasteries were prime targets for marauding Muslim armies who attacked them to seize their riches.

Meanwhile, the once-fragmented Brahmanism and other Indian religions evolved into an increasingly unified and sophisticated Hinduism. In India, Tantric Buddhism deteriorated and its remnants were absorbed into Hinduism by about 1200 AD. However, Vajrayana still survived in Tibet, where Buddhism was embraced in the 7th Century.

While Buddhism was dying out in India, Mahayana Buddhism had spread into China, Japan and Korea. The reformer's spirit remained active in Mahayana Buddhism, and today it takes many forms. Some still emphasize the "Buddhism for the common person" approach to practice.

As I mentioned above, all these different points of view can seem very confusing to someone just getting acquainted with Buddhism, and one might regret that the Buddhist community has been splintered by disputes over the years, especially when some of those disputes may seem irrelevant to contemporary Western Buddhists.

For example, to someone just trying to figure out what they're supposed to be doing when meditating or get a basic understanding of the Four Noble Truths, the question "Should I practice in order to become a bodhisattva or an arahant?" can seem pretty pointless.

But when we consider the many forms Buddhism now takes and the many points of view that have survived so many generations of teaching and practice, we see the benefit of this variety. Just as there is no such thing as an "average" human, there is no need for a one-size-fits-all Buddhism, and different ways of relating to the dharma will resonate with different people.

As we approach these teachings, it's good to have a clear idea of the relationship between *practice* and *faith* as they relate to Buddhist practice. At times, studying and practicing the dharma can be frustrating, confusing or overwhelming. A little faith can go a long way to keep one from losing patience and giving up.

Faith is a controversial topic for many American Buddhists. Because of experiences they've had in the past, some people tend to be wary about anything that sounds too religious. However, faith is necessary to Buddhist practice. But Buddhist faith is very different from what we might mean when we talk about faith in other religions.

When I was about 30 years old, I was doing a lot of triathlons. I remember one race in particular, and I remember standing on the sand of Panama City Beach, looking out at the ocean. A series of buoys marked off a 1.5-mile swim course shaped like an elongated diamond—I could see them lined up one after another, stretching out toward the horizon. A few volunteers sat on paddle boards near the farthest point, almost 2/3 of a mile away; they looked tiny, almost invisible bobbing up and down among the waves.

In this race, I was to swim that 1.5 miles, then bike another 60 through the Florida panhandle before running another 13.1 miles through Panama City. As I stood there looking out to sea, I suddenly felt the reality of all those miles stretching out in front of me. I was surrounded by hundreds of fellow triathletes. Many of them looked out at the Gulf of Mexico, and I'm sure some were thinking the same thought I had at that moment— "I must be out of my damn mind!"

That's *doubt*.

There are five hindrances that block the path of spiritual progress, and doubt is among them. The antidote to doubt is *faith*. The doubt we're talking about is not healthy skepticism—the Buddha encouraged that. Likewise, this faith is not unquestioning acceptance—it's not blind faith. Buddhist faith is more like the kind of faith that gets you through a challenging situation like a long triathlon.

If I'd kept my doubt that morning, I'd have bailed out of the triathlon before the starter pistol sounded. However, I remembered my faith—not the faith athletes mean when they thank God for helping them win the Olympic gold medal, but faith in the swim-bike-run dharma. I had read what coaches and elite athletes said about training for triathlons; I had learned from more experienced triathletes; and I done the training and realized the results in growing levels of strength and endurance.

There was more than just sheer force of will or strong-hearted belief involved. I had done some research, found wisdom and applied that wisdom to my training, which is the Buddhist view of how faith works.

There is an old parable that symbolizes the relationship between Buddhist faith and wisdom: A dwarf and a giant somehow encounter one another in the forest. Both are miserable, because neither can get where they want to go. The giant is strong and long-legged, but his eyesight is so terrible he can only manage to thrash around aimlessly in the woods. The dwarf has the eyesight of a hawk, but he can barely walk; he can see where he needs to go, but his legs just won't carry him there.

"I have an idea," says the dwarf. "Why don't I ride on your shoulders? With my vision and your strength, we can go anywhere we want to go."

My teacher on the Mahayana side, Rev. Koyo Kubose, suggests using code words and capping phrases—a word or short phrase that sums up a principle of the dharma in a way that is personally meaningful. One of his favorites is the phrase, "Keep going." I like it so much that I co-opted it for my own use. It has become a very simple statement of my faith: When in doubt, "Keep going."

Before one can keep going, however, one must *get* going. There is an element of faith in that, too. That's where the story of the Buddha comes into play: Siddhartha Gautama was a human being, like us, who freed himself from suffering by doing things we can do. We can follow his example, and armed with that little bit of faith, we can get going.

When starting a Buddhist practice, seek guidance from experienced people who have been where you are and gone where you want to go. Hear or read the dharma, and then analyze what you heard to make sure it makes sense and to make sure you understand how to put the teaching to practice. Then practice the dharma and realize the results.

More than once, I have looked at my own mind and seen the buoy of enlightenment bobbing unimaginably far off shore, and more than once I've observed my breath rising and falling and thought, "Who the heck am I trying to kid?"

Without faith, that would be the end of it. Fortunately, the Buddha left us his training plan, which he realized and taught to others who realized it in turn. Now, almost 2,600 years after he lived, I have the good fortune of knowing teachers who have been where I am and gone where I want to go and are willing to share their knowledge with me. All that remains is to practice.

As we practice, we can see day to day where the practice has taken us so far, and faith can help us continue developing more wisdom, more compassion and more serenity, bringing us a little closer each day to liberation.

All we have to do is keep going.

GRADUAL INSTRUCTION

A number of people have said to me, "I really like what the Dalai Lama says"—or Thich Nhat Hanh, or whatever other famous Buddhist they've seen, heard or read—"but I could never be a Buddhist, because I can't sit still long enough to meditate!"

Such a statement reveals two fairly significant misunderstandings: First, it reflects a misunderstanding of meditation, which we'll see later. But there is also a misconception about Buddhism that's very prevalent in the US that that Buddhism and meditation are synonymous. In fact, many of the world's Buddhists don't meditate. And meditation—at least in the sense of spending long periods sitting cross-legged on the floor—is not essential to Buddhist practice.

I do meditate and encourage meditation, and I will discuss meditation at some length later on. However, the Buddha revealed his teachings in a sequence of instructions with meditation coming near the end, there are a number of ways one should prepare one's mind before jumping into meditation practice.

Dana

On one chilly Thanksgiving evening, I built a fire in the fireplace. As my wife and I relaxed by the fire, I thought about the events of the day. She and some other Volusia Buddhist Fellowship members wanted to donate holiday meals to a local organization that works with families in crisis, so that day a few of us had gone to a local barbecue place to pick up a couple of large turkeys with all the trimmings for the families who were spending the holiday in their shelter.

The shelter director was very happy to see us, of course, and thanked us profusely. Surprisingly, perhaps, I felt an overwhelming desire to thank him. That feeling of gratitude returned as I sat by the fire, and for some reason, it reminded me about the *Fire Sermon* the Buddha gave to the 1,000 hermits just after his enlightenment.

> *Whatever arises from causes and conditions is aflame with the fire of greed, the fire of anger and the fire of delusion.*

> *Thus it is aflame with sorrows, aflame with pain, burning with distress and despair.*

I gazed into the fire and tried to imagine what it was like to sit there among 1,000 matted-haired hermits hearing the Buddha preach this fiery sermon.

The ancient Indians believed fire didn't end when it went out. A fire, when burning, was clinging to its fuel; when the fuel was used up, the fire became "unbound" and dispersed through the universe. Likewise the mind, when it is no longer fueled by craving and aversion, can become unbound from the cycle of conditioning much like a flame unbinds from a log as it turns to ash.

The Buddha often talked about the importance of giving as the first step on a spiritual path that led to that unbinding. It occurred to me that the shelter director had made it very easy for me to do that which the Buddha said we must do if we want to attain that unbinding—to practice letting go.

When the Buddha taught, he often began by talking about the value of giving. He said if one truly comes to understand the value of giving, one will not want to take a single meal without sharing food with others.

Giving—or dana, the Pali/Sanskrit word you hear in a Buddhist context—is a prerequisite to the process of awakening. Understanding the value of giving is the foundation on which the spiritual path is constructed; every theme that follows depends on the practitioner's ability to let go of something they think they can't do without but which actually creates problems for them.

Dana is first on the list of virtuous qualities to be perfected. It's also considered a highly *meritorious* action. I want to explain this idea of merit, because it's hard to grasp the importance of dana without talking about merit.

The concept of merit derives from the law of karma: If you do good things, you get a good result; if you do bad things, you get a bad result. Thus merit is sort of like what you commonly hear referred to as "good karma."

A lot of American Buddhists shy away from the topic of merit, perhaps because it sounds like there's some cosmic scorecard where merit accumulations are tracked; if you accumulate enough, you'll get a better rebirth or some kind of good fortune. On the surface, the Asian tradition of merit-making can seem a little superstitious.

However, the Buddha equated merit with happiness. If you accumulate merit, it means you're accumulating causes for happiness, your own happiness and the happiness of others. The more merit you make, the closer you move toward freedom from the stuff that keeps you stuck doing the things that cause you unhappiness.

We talked about merit in a meeting one evening, and Greg, one of our members, found a great analogy for it. "It's like going to the gym," he said. "You don't see the results right away, but you know they're accumulating" so eventually you'll experience weight loss and fitness gains.

I think to shy away from the practice of making merit is a mistake. Westerners are attracted to Buddhism because of its rationality, and they approach their practice intellectually. That's okay, but Buddhism is also a practice of the heart. One can easily get bogged down in Buddhist head games, but making merit comes from the heart. Anyone can do it without studying sutras for years or mastering advanced meditation techniques.

Greed, hatred and delusion cause much our stress in life. Dana counteracts greed and hatred. Further, because the practice demonstrates to us directly that letting go of things can lead to happiness, dana also helps us stop clinging to our delusions.

Think about greed for a moment. I think you could say greed is the idea that having *more* will lead to happiness. If I have money and I'm not happy, I must need more money, more sports cars, a more expensive Rolex and so on. If our lives are built around greed, we probably don't think we can get happiness from giving something away, because then we'd have *less*, and thus less happiness.

So the mental mechanism of greed works from the position, "There is *never enough*." When you give, however, you put yourself in a position of wealth. The gift is proof that you have more than enough—you have enough to share. Thus dana directly counteracts the "never enough" mindset of greed.

The Buddha once went to ask for alms in a village that had been hit hard with famine. Some Brahmins criticized him for that—it was shameful, they said, to knowingly beg for food from people who barely had enough for themselves.

However, the Buddha explained that he'd gone there deliberately. The spirit of giving was much needed at such times, he said, because when there are shortages of necessities, people will hoard, steal or otherwise harm one another to get more and keep whatever they have. He felt people needed to be reminded of the value of sharing—only when given a chance to share would they experience their true wealth.

We learn from the practice of dana that we can get real happiness from giving some of our wealth to others in need. It's counterintuitive—we think we get happiness from having more, but we learn we actually get happiness from giving more away. In the process, we open up to the idea that there may be other counterintuitive ways to happiness.

For example, sitting still and doing nothing doesn't sound very exciting, so most people probably wouldn't think that's a path to happiness. Meditation, however, is largely a matter of sitting still and doing nothing. While doing that "nothing," you learn to let go of other things that arise, and you get to a kind of happiness you otherwise probably don't get to experience very often.

Dana doesn't have to mean big material donations, by the way. The Buddha said, "Even if a person rinses out a bowl or cup and throws the water into a pond thinking, 'May whatever animals live here feed on this,' that would be a source of merit."

When you give, you develop a giving mind. When you open your heart to the idea that sharing whatever you have brings you happiness, you begin to see the dichotomy between "my" happiness and the happiness of others dissolving.

After he would teach people about giving, the Buddha would proceed to a discussion of moral restraint, asking them to avoid killing, stealing, irresponsible sexual activity, harmful speech, and misusing intoxicants. To vow to practice such compassionate, non-harming behavior is also a gift, he said. You're creating a safer environment, so you're giving the other beings in your world a share in that safety.

As I mentioned above, anger is a cause of suffering. Often, when I talk to a group about the need to abandon anger, people will argue with me. We find it pretty easy to see how other people's anger is a problem. Our own anger, however, seems quite justified. "*Your* anger is a problem," we think. "But *my* anger—well, I deserve to be angry about this terrible injustice, which won't be put right unless I'm mad about it."

When we look at it closely, however, we can usually see that however justifiable our anger, it never makes matters any better. Also, if we stop and experience what's happening in our bodies when we're angry, we see that our response to anger is very real, physical suffering.

While we may want to cling to our anger, we can try instead to practice non-anger as a form of generosity. Despite wanting to keep it and treasure it, we can let our anger go and give the object of our anger freedom from the physical expressions anger usually takes. You give yourself a gift at the same time: If you can manage to let your anger go, you'll feel a lot better.

Meditation may also be seen as a kind of gift to others. By trying to understand your greed, anger and delusion and bring them under control, other people will benefit from your practice. Sharing the dharma is a great gift. Some can do that by teaching while others do it by participating in and supporting a spiritual community.

I mentioned above the idea that when you do good, you get a good result, and that good result is represented by the idea of merit. One of the things Buddhists do as part of our practice is give merit away—which is another act of generosity. That keeps us from clinging to the idea that we get something in return for our generosity and thus keeps the giving free from selfishness.

You might wonder, "Does it truly benefit others when I share my merit?" Again, that might seem a little superstitious, as if you're dipping into your storehouse of merit to spread it around. However, sharing your blessings helps you develop your giving nature. What greater gift could you give?

Studying the dharma is a meritorious act. If you like, take a moment and dedicate the merit you have accumulated by reading about dana and considering how to develop your own giving nature. Just sit comfortably for a moment, close your eyes or otherwise look inward and cultivate the intention to share your blessings with others:

> *May all beings always live happily*
> *Free from animosity.*
> *May all share in the blessings*
> *That spring from the good we have done.*

Sila

Just as Buddhist psychology anticipated 20th century cognitive therapy by pointing out that our suffering is largely the product of our thinking, so Buddhist ethics anticipated that of the 20th century existentialists by 2,500 years or more by pointing out the connection between our existence, our will and our actions.

Buddhist ethics begins with the idea of karma—action and the result of action. However, Buddhism extends the idea of a simple individual karma to include the concept of interdependence, the realization that individual karma is affected by and effects interpersonal karma and the karma generated by the universe.

Therefore, we are all related by karma. Each of us, and every other being around us, exists because of causes and conditions, and each will end because of causes and conditions. Those causes and conditions are inextricably interwoven: As one Theravada chant says, all beings are related by karma. Thus, while each being is the owner of his or her own karma, whatever affects one affects all.

During the Buddha's time, the law of karma was used to explain why some people were "better born" than others and to justify a rigid caste system. However, Buddhism added the concept of individual responsibility, explaining that good actions led to good results and bad actions to bad results.

When we extend this idea to include interdependence, we see we are responsible not only for ourselves, but that humankind and the universe itself become what we create with our actions. Thus each of us has a hand in the creation of humankind and the world we live in. So to the question "Is humankind ultimately good or evil?" or "Is the universe heaven or hell?" we can respond "It is what we create."

Existentialist Jean-Paul Sartre pointed out that a human is defined by his or her willful actions—in Buddhist terms by his or her karma. It follows that humankind is defined by the actions of its collective individuals. If I act out of kindness and compassion—if I resolve to lead all beings to enlightenment, no matter how numberless those beings and no matter how daunting that challenge seems—then that karma will tend to direct my world toward a higher spiritual level.

In Mahayana Buddhism, the goal of practice isn't personal enlightenment—becoming an arahant—but the enlightenment of all beings. When one formally goes for refuge in the Buddha, therefore, part of that process will involve taking the Bodhisattva vow, making the commitment to work for spiritual ease on behalf of all beings.

Some might say an idea like the Bodhisattva vow is unworkable and even futile. For a response, however, we might look to another existentialist. In his essay *The Myth of Sisyphus*, Albert Camus compared such human efforts to the life of Sisyphus, a character from Greek mythology who was doomed to spend each day rolling a massive stone to the top of a hill only to see it roll back down again. Is the absurdity of this struggle a reason to give up? Camus says it is not.

"This universe…seems to him neither sterile nor futile," he says. "Each atom of that stone, each mineral flake of that night-filled mountain in itself forms a world. The struggle itself toward the heights is enough to fill a man's heart. One must imagine Sisyphus happy." (Camus)

As Buddhists, we approach an ethical question without a set of hard and fast rules engraved in stone by a higher authority. Rather, we are guided by compassion. When the Buddha gave his first sermon setting the wheel of dharma in motion, he laid out a path of practice that includes right speech, right actions and right livelihood. Thus the Buddhist concept of ethics or morality, *sila*, begins with the commitment to avoid harming other beings.

In practice, this involves five main guidelines for ethical behavior:

(1) to refrain from killing
(2) to refrain from taking what is not freely given
(3) to refrain from harmful speech—false, idle or harsh speech
(4) to refrain from harmful sexual activity
(5) and to refrain from using intoxicants that might impair one's

mindfulness and thus lead one to harm.

These are not commandments—there is no deity saying "Thou shalt not" do these things. Rather, they are considered training precepts. When you take the precepts, rather than vowing to obey a set of rules you vow to *set your mind on* abandoning killing, stealing, and so on. So the value of the precepts is twofold: By abandoning uncompassionate actions, you are giving others an incrementally safer, happier world, and you are also training your mind to cultivate compassion.

When I first began learning about Buddhism, I was impressed with the idea that its morality came not in commandments but in the form of a vow. As a kid growing up in a Baptist family, the thought of obeying the Ten Commandments seemed overwhelming, and these rules often seemed to be interpreted and applied arbitrarily. Vowing to train in compassionate behavior, however, seemed relatively liberating. At the same time, it invites each of us to accept personal responsibility for our ethical choices.

Taking personal responsibility to act with compassion does not always leave us with black-and-white alternatives, however. It can be difficult to determine a near-perfect compassionate path when reality presents us with an ethical dilemma. Therefore, although we should strive to perfect our ethical behavior, we can never expect to *be* perfect.

Heaven

One Thursday, a newcomer showed up at the Buddhist meeting at Tomoka Correctional Institution. While he was spending some time in lockup, someone had passed him a book about Tibetan Buddhism. It resonated with him, so he decided to attend one of our meetings. At the end of the meeting, we dedicate our practice, sharing the blessings with all other beings.

That dedication takes the form of a prayer, and the new guy asked me, "Are you praying to Buddha?"

Another inmate from our group answered: No, he said, the Buddha was a human being, just like us. We don't pray to him.

"Then who are you praying to?" the new guy wondered.

This is a very good question. Buddhism isn't about the worship of any particular being and we don't call on God for our liberation, yet we do chant and say verses that sound a lot like prayer. So if salvation doesn't come to us from a deity outside ourselves, to whom are we praying, and for what?

During the '60s and '70s, there were a lot of young people going to Southeast Asia to learn about Buddhism. Many ended up studying with a Thai monk named Ajahn Chah. "You ask God for salvation," Ajahn Chah would say. "That's like going to the doctor and saying, 'Doctor, I'm sick—would you please take some medicine so I'll feel better?' That won't work, will it? You have to take the medicine yourself."

If you asked most religious people to sum up their religion in a few words, they'd probably state it in terms of a belief. But the Buddha was once asked to explain his religion briefly, and this is what he said: "Do good; avoid doing evil; train your mind." You can do that while believing in any god—or no god at all.

I often talk to people who are drawn to Buddhism because it makes sense on that kind of rational level. The Buddha was often referred to as a great physician, who was treating the disease of human suffering. So a lot of people get turned off by the religion of their heritage, but they try meditation or read something about Buddhism, and they see how it can help them overcome some of the things they're doing to create problems for themselves and others.

Sometimes, such a person will start to read about and practice Buddhist teachings, and then they hit this wall. They find prayers, and references to gods and devas and demons and ghosts. They start encountering topics like karma and rebirth, and find out there are Buddhist heavens and Buddhist hells. And suddenly this religion that seemed so sensible starts to look like it might be just as full of superstition and require just as much faith as any other. However, we can demystify that fairly easily if we think in terms of the idea of a Sacred Story.

Here's an example of what I mean. When Siddhartha's mother, Mahamaya, was about to give birth to him, she traveled with her retinue toward her parents' home to have the child. She stopped in a garden along the way, in Lumbini. And there she reached up and grasped the branch of a Sala tree and gave birth.

The infant Buddha-to-be, so the story says, took seven steps, with lotus blossoms springing up from his footsteps. He then pointed to the sky and said, "I alone am the World-Honored One," meaning the person who could liberate humanity from suffering.

Probably few people believe that story to be literally true. However, it's more than a myth. I think for most Asian Buddhists, this is a sacred story. It's not true in any journalistic or historic sense and it's not a metaphor, exactly; rather, the story itself is a vehicle for what we might call *spiritual* truths. These are truths of the heart, not truths of the head. We don't have to believe in them—we just try to live them.

Ideas like heavens and hells fall into this category of spiritual truth. In the west, we think of heaven and hell as sort of a reward/punishment concept, and we're rewarded for believing in the right thing by getting to go to heaven. And if we don't believe in the right thing, we have to go to hell. In Buddhism, heavens and hells are considered more like mental states.

There's an old Japanese story about a Samurai who bursts into a monastery demanding that an old monk immediately teach him all about heaven and hell. When the old monk refuses, the samurai angrily draws his sword, preparing to kill the monk.

The monk looks at him calmly. "There open the gates of hell," he says.

The samurai realizes his anger is, indeed, hell, and he sheaths his sword.

"And there open the gates of heaven," the monk says.

In Buddhism, heaven and hell are the result of action. Since we are interdependent, our karmas, our actions, are interrelated. Thus we are responsible not only for ourselves, but humankind and the universe itself become what we create with our actions (karma). So to the question 'Is humankind ultimately good or evil?' or 'Is the universe heaven or hell?' we can respond 'It is what we create.'

Note, heaven and hell are not God's creations—they're ours. There are gods in Buddhism, but they're not considered the way to liberation, although some Buddhist traditions call on Bodhisattvas in heavens for help. However, when you start looking at Buddhist versions of heaven and hell, you find some interesting sacred stories and spiritual truths that you can use when you consider what sort of heaven or hell you're building.

The first interesting thing you find is that in Buddhist cosmology, there is no eternal heaven and hell. Beings are born into a heaven or hell—or as a human or animal—based on karmic cause and effect. Once the karma is exhausted, then life in that realm ends. So even if you do tons and tons of good and get born as a deva in a heaven, that life will eventually come to an end.

There are about three dozen realms of existence in Buddhism, by the way. There are several formless realms for people who pass away while meditating in very highly refined meditative states. Then there are 16 heavenly realms where the devas live. The highest of those are the Pure Lands, which are accessible only to those who have reached a certain level of awakening.

Then there are 11 realms in which experience is dominated by the senses, and that includes the human realm, animal realm, some of the lower heavens, and the hells.

We really don't need to worry about whether these states actually exist or are metaphorical. The point, really, is that unless we break free of the cycle of suffering, we're doomed to wander aimlessly from one state to another.

I've learned from my Buddhist practice that if I'm having trouble with belief, I should shift from trying to believe in the concept to practicing it. Usually, then, I figure out what teaching is contained in the concept. So consider, for example, the Hungry Ghosts who inhabit one of the hells.

People who spent their lives in greed, giving in to craving and addiction are said to be reborn as Hungry Ghosts. Because of their long, skinny necks, huge bellies and tiny mouths, these ghosts are constantly hungry but can never get enough to eat. And when they do find good food, it turns into something disgusting as they eat it.

Look around at people whose lives are controlled by greed and you will see hungry ghosts—people who, no matter how much they get, never feel as if they have enough. Or look at an addict or an alcoholic—once they start living by that craving, it's never sated.

Even a relatively benign craving like chocolate can be harmful. If you eat too much of it, it can lead to health problems. So that nice food you were going to enjoy will turn into something disgusting if you excessively indulge your craving.

Sometimes such cravings are represented in sacred stories about anthropomorphic figures like Mara or his daughters. The word Mara actually has a few different meanings. There's one representation of him as the king of the sensual realm, where his main activity seems to be making life difficult for monks and nuns. There are also references to Maras as a class of deities, and at times the personification of death is called Mara. Most often, Mara is kind of an allegory for the power of temptation.

There are a half-dozen scriptural encounters between the Buddha or Buddha-to-be and Mara. In one, for example, Gautama is nearing the point where he'll reach enlightenment, and Mara tries to talk him out of it, saying, "the path is too rough."

The Buddha answers that Mara is waging a battle, using things like desire, boredom and hunger as his armies. But Mara will lose, he says:

Better I die in battle now
Than choose to live on in defeat.
For I have faith and energy,
And I have wisdom too.
Your row upon row of squadrons,
Which the world cannot defeat,
I shall now break with wisdom
As a stone breaks a clay pot.[3]

Later, the Buddha-to-be sits beneath the tree, determined not to rise until he has reached enlightenment. Mara tries to stop him with his armies, but he is undeterred. Then Mara calls into question whether he's worthy of being a Buddha. This time, Gautama reaches down to touch the ground and calls on the earth as his witness. Soon afterward, he is enlightened.

These stories are inspirational descriptions of the Buddha's

---

[3] Padhaana Sutta

determination to defeat the mechanism of suffering, and by showing us his encounters with Mara they highlight the heroism of his inner struggle. Maras are the demons that keep us from realizing our true nature, our Buddha nature. Since each of us is under the sway of various Maras, this story shows us that we, too, are heroes doing battle with the demons of greed, anger and delusion.

All religion has an element of faith and an element of practice, but in Buddhism, practice comes first. If your religion is based on a belief in God, you might consider prayer a chance to talk to God, to be heard by God, even to ask God for something—to let you keep your job, for soldiers to come home quickly from war or for hurricanes and earthquakes to pass us by.

In the Buddhist view, that's dualistic: It implies there's a thing called "me" over here and a thing called "God" over there. We tend to think of this "me" or "self" as something solid and enduring, when really it's more like a wave on the ocean.

If you look at a wave, you see it's made up from a combination of matter and energy, of water and wind, the moon's pull and things like that. If you tried to isolate that wave from the ocean—if you could take one of those aircraft they use to fight forest fires and scoop it up in a big bucket— you wouldn't have a wave. You'd have a bunch of water, maybe some seaweed and plankton, salt and other dissolved minerals, but you wouldn't have a wave at all. You can't have that wave without the ocean and all the causes and conditions that created it.

We're a lot like that wave. We flow a little more slowly, perhaps, but we're still flowing. Since you started reading this page, you've been breathing. Molecules that you would have said were "me" are now something else. Maybe you've read something that caused you to drop one idea and pick up another, so thoughts you would have claimed as "my beliefs" are no longer yours. As long as you eat, breathe, think and live, you're like that wave. What you think of as "me" is a bunch of causes and conditions coming together, falling apart, coming together, falling apart, rising and falling like the breath.

Buddhist practice, in part, is about realizing our oneness with that flow of causes and conditions. That is where we find liberation—where we find peace. Prayer becomes a means to that experience—it is a conduit to our spirituality. You could even say spirituality is what happens when the wave becomes aware of the ocean.

So to a Buddhist, a prayer is more of a question than a request. We're not praying so that we can be heard, we pray so that we can hear the dharma. "Dharma" is an interesting word—it can refer to the teachings of the Buddha, or it can refer to the Universal Truth, the ground of being. Praying so that we can hear the dharma, I think, is essentially the same thing as listening to the voice of God.

Ajahn Chah was also famous for saying that looking for peace is like looking for a turtle with a mustache—You won't find it. "But if your heart is ready, peace will come looking for you," he would explain. To a Buddhist, praying is a way to make the heart ready for peace to come.

So when you pray, consider not thinking of your prayer as a doorbell you ring in hopes that someone will answer. Instead, think of your prayer as a key that opens the door so you can experience dharma yourself, directly, whatever dharma means to you.

Drawbacks of Sensual Pleasure and Benefits of Renunciation

One of the cable channels was running a *Twilight Zone* marathon, and my wife and I sat down to watch a few episodes of the old shows, including one from 1960 entitled "A Nice Place to Visit." The plot revolved around a criminal sociopath named Rocky Valentine, who suddenly awoke to find himself in a nice apartment with a kindly, rotund butler named Pip.

With some prodding from Pip, Valentine comes to realize he has died from a policeman's gunshot, and the butler is his guide to the afterlife. Recalling his evil past, Valentine assumes horrible things are going to start happening to him any minute. To his surprise and delight, however, he finds that all he has to do is ask for something—a lavish dinner, a million dollars, a beautiful woman—and it is his. If he wants to go out, a fancy car appears outside to take him nightclubbing. Whenever he gambles, he wins big.

Valentine is confused, however—how does he rate this wonderful afterlife? Perhaps he did something really good that he has forgotten. He asks Pip if there are account books somewhere of his deeds, but a visit to the Hall of Records reveals nothing in his file but a long list of sins. He shrugs it off and decides to enjoy what surely must have been a mistake— that he will live eternally in such wonderful circumstances.

But eventually the never-ending wonderfulness of it all begins to wear thin. With every meal a gourmet feast, the food all begins to taste the same. Gambling is no fun if it's impossible to lose. Although their looks never fade, the women that surround him lose their charm. Valentine begins to get bored, and the boredom grows moment by moment.

Finally, in desperation, Valentine decides he'd be better off without all that luxury and ease. He begs Pip to let him leave. "I don't belong in heaven," he says. "I want to go to the other place!"

"Heaven, Mr. Valentine?" Pip replies. "Whatever gave you the idea you were in heaven? This *is* the other place!"

In a few days in hell, Valentine has learned much about the drawbacks of desire. A lot of times, you'll hear someone say that the Buddha said suffering was caused by desire. That's sort of true, but not exactly. The Buddha actually said the root of stress and suffering is craving, meaning taking desire beyond the point of preference to the point of "need" and mistakenly believing that getting what we desire will give us happiness. As Valentine learned, any happiness that is contingent on externals is inevitably disappointing.

Buddhism is no Pollyanna philosophy—the objective isn't to feel good all the time, but to accept life's ups and downs. Life contains suffering, and we can't transcend it by pretending it's not there or by trying to escape it through sense objects. Siddhartha realized this when he saw that regardless of his material wealth, he would still experience dukkha.

There is a story in the sutras about a monk, Ven. Bhaddiya, who had been a king before he ordained. Ven. Bhaddiya would go into the forest, sit at the base of a tree and start meditating. And while meditating, he would repeatedly exclaim, "What bliss! What bliss!"

Other monks heard that. Some of them thought maybe he was crazy, but after some discussion, they decided he was probably recalling the bliss of kingship, reliving his life of comfort during his meditation. So they went to the Buddha and told him this.

The Buddha said, "Go call him—tell him the teacher wishes to see him." When Ven. Bhaddiya came to see the Buddha, he asked, "Is it true, Bhaddiya that, on going to a forest, you sit at the foot of a tree and repeatedly exclaim, 'What bliss! What bliss!'?"

Bhaddiya said it was true.

"What do you have in mind while you're exclaiming, 'What bliss! What bliss!'?" the Buddha asked.

Bhaddiya explained that life as a king was very good—as a king, he had ridden everywhere on the finest elephants, eaten the best food from the best tableware, and so on. But at the same time, he had lived in fear. He had to have guards around his home and at his side when he traveled in order to protect those fine sensual comforts. Thus he lived, he said, agitated, distrustful and afraid.

When he ordained, he had renounced all those material comforts. Rather than riding in high style, he now walked. Rather than eating the best kingly food, he ate whatever was put in his simple alms bowl. However, he had come out ahead, he said. In exchange for the bliss of material pleasures that were fleeting, unstable, and stressful, he received freedom from distrust, freedom from agitation and freedom from fear.

"I live unconcerned, unruffled, my wants satisfied, with my mind like a wild deer," he said. "This is what I have in mind when I repeatedly exclaim, 'What bliss! What bliss!'"

We can't all ordain, of course, but one doesn't have to take the robes in order to experience the benefits of renunciation. For example, we might set aside a time for a personal spiritual retreat.

The idea of a spiritual retreat goes all the way back to the Buddha's time. When he was alive, his monks would spend the rainy season, which in India lasts roughly from mid-July to mid-October, assembled with him at a monastery, listening to teachings. Since all these monks were assembled in one place for three months, householders would also come to the monastery and listen to the dharma.

After the Buddha's death, monks continued to assemble at monasteries during the rains, and householder Buddhists would still come to the monasteries to listen to the dharma. Today, Southeast Asian Buddhist communities observe the rains, Vassa, with special observances, including a series of dharma talks that begins with the sutra Setting the Wheel of Dharma in Motion and going through a review of the key Buddhist teachings.

Earlier, we mentioned the five main precepts. These are vows of ethical behavior that help us train the mind to avoid harming others: to refrain from killing, stealing, using harmful speech, engaging in harmful sexual actions and becoming intoxicated so you lose your mindfulness.

During Vassa, some Buddhists will also observe more austere precepts. These more stringent vows are the precepts of renunciation, so we also refrain from eating after noon; all sexual activity; music, dancing, makeup and jewelry; and lazing around in bed.

Sometimes people refer to this as "Buddhist Lent," but that's not really very accurate. These austerities aren't about identifying with suffering—the discomfort is really pretty mild. Rather, renunciation is about experiencing the deeper happiness that comes when we learn to transcend our attachment to things that we think we need in order to feel good. Practicing renunciation is a way to experience a trade-off like Ven. Bhaddiya described—we swap short-term gratification for long-term good.

Renouncing an addiction is kind of a good example of how that works. I smoked for a long time. Smoking, for me, was pleasurable. I would sometimes smoke a pipe, and I enjoyed selecting nice tobacco, and the smell and the sensation was pleasant. I also smoked cigarettes, and one of the best feelings of the day came in the morning when I'd light that first one and get that nicotine rush. When I refrained from smoking even for a little while, I'd have a very unpleasant craving arise, but a few drags could eliminate that. Smoking helped me cope with boredom, anxiety and any number of other adversities.

As Ven. Bhaddiya put it, that kind of pleasure is fleeting, unstable, and stressful. However, there was always this idea that "*This* smoke is going to satisfy me." You have this sense that somehow this cigarette or this bowl of tobacco is going make everything okay. You're not thinking, "This one is going to feel good, and then I'll feel bad again." You just focus on the first half—the "feel good" part.

At some point, though, you realize, "Yes, for the next hour or so, I'll feel okay. But then I'm going to want another one. And even after the cigarette is gone, the smoky smell lingers, the toxins are damaging my body, and so on." When you realize that the disadvantages outweigh the advantages, you resolve to trade away the short-term "good" for the longer-term "better."

If you then resolve to quit smoking, you'll have to deal with the cravings that arise. Instead of giving in or temporarily suppressing a craving, you try to abandon it. Once you attempt to abandon a craving, it comes out into the open, full-blown, with all its rationalizations and exhortations to give in to it. When that happens, you can remind yourself that the cravings that arise, like the relief that comes from smoking, are also impermanent. The craving is dukkha, but giving into the craving would create much *more* dukkha.

Eventually, we get to experience a little bit of the peace that occurs when we're freed from the craving. If you succeed in quitting smoking, you will have traded the short-term refuge of smoking for the long-term refuge of non-smoking and the freedom and health benefits that come with it. Similarly, the practice of renunciation is about trading short-term comforts for long-term spiritual growth and greater spiritual ease.

Whether you do it for three months, for one day a week, during an annual retreat or during 20 minutes of meditation in the morning, practicing renunciation is a way to work with your desires—to see which ones create problems and which ones you can release, and then to let go of the problem ones.

A monastic life or even a long retreat or renunciation period may never be appropriate for you. But maybe, as you go through your life, you can set aside some special time to think about what's really important, to look for opportunities to let go of craving and to simplify your life a little. In the process, you might trade some of the cares and stresses of everyday life for the chance to find a truer form of happiness.

The Four Noble Truths

The core teachings of Buddhism come from the teaching he gave to his ascetic companions at the Deer Park, where he laid out the Four Noble Truths and the Noble Eightfold Path. In most cases, however, the Buddha would only give this teaching to newcomers to the dharma after explaining the importance of giving, the need for ethical restraint, the workings of heaven, hell and karma, the drawbacks of sensual pleasure and the benefits to be gained from renunciation.

We discussed this teaching briefly in Part One, but I want to summarize it again here before we delve more deeply into it in the coming chapters.

The First Noble Truth is often translated as "All life is suffering." Of course, we know not all life is suffering—sometimes there's suffering, and sometimes there isn't. Actually, "suffering" is not a great translation for the Pali word "dukkha," which includes all the stresses and dissatisfactions that are associated with instability and impermanence. Here's what the Buddha said in Setting the Wheel of Dharma in Motion:

Now this, monks, is the noble truth of stress (dukkha): Birth is stressful, aging is stressful, death is stressful; sorrow, lamentation, pain, distress, and despair are stressful; association with the unloved is stressful, separation from the loved is stressful, not getting what is wanted is stressful. In short, the five clinging aggregates are stressful.

And this, monks, is the noble truth of the origination of stress: the craving that makes for further becoming, craving for sensual pleasure, craving for becoming, craving for non-becoming.

And this, monks, is the noble truth of the cessation of stress: the complete fading, cessation, renunciation, abandonment, release and letting go of that very craving.

And this, monks, is the noble truth of the way leading to the cessation of stress: the Noble Eightfold Path—right view, right resolve, right speech, right action, right livelihood, right effort, right mindfulness, right concentration.[4]

As we begin to consider how to put that teaching into practice, I'm going to reword it with the form used by the Bright Dawn Center for Oneness Buddhism.

The First Noble Truth is that afflictions and difficulties are facts of life. As long as the five aggregates of physical form plus feelings, perceptions, karma-conditioning and awareness are still "clinging" to one another, we will encounter stress. Thus all living beings are subject to adversity.

The Second Noble Truth is that in response to such afflictions and difficulties, cravings and emotions arise. Because of our karma-conditioning, we will often experience responses to difficulties with attachments and aversions such as anger, delusion and greed.

The Third Noble Truth is that such cravings and emotions can be wisely harnessed and directed. Once we understand that our stress is caused by attachment and aversion, we can begin to transcend it; instead of letting our cravings and emotions create suffering, we can

---

[4] Dhammacakkappavattana Sutta

abandon them or cultivate more helpful mental and emotional responses.

The Fourth Noble Truth is that harnessing the emotions that arise in response to life's afflictions leads to enlightened living, the Eightfold Path:

Right View: To understand and realize the true nature of life.

Right Resolve: To direct our deepest aspirations toward charity, non-violence and selfless concern for others.

Right Speech: To speak truthfully, kindly, and courteously to all.

Right Action: To act in a way that is peaceful, benevolent, and does no harm to others.

Right Livelihood: To earn one's living in such a way as to avoid harmful consequences.

Right Effort: To strive diligently to overcome anger, greed, and ignorance.

Right Mindfulness: To remember and cherish the qualities of wisdom and compassion.

Right Concentration: To set one's mind on fully becoming One with the reality of life in all its forms in the eternal now.

The Path of Practice: Wisdom; Compassion; Serenity

I spent a Labor Day weekend at a Zen retreat organized by a Unitarian Universalist church that had arranged for a roshi (Zen master) to come to Florida and teach. The church's pastor was a Zen student himself, but most of the others who attended were fairly new to meditation.

The retreat started on Friday evening, and the pastor explained the schedule after dinner. As is common in Zen retreats there would be a work period every day. In addition to whatever tasks we did during that period, each of us had also been assigned a turn washing the dishes after a meal.

He also explained the idea of work as a spiritual practice. "It's like Thich Nhat Hanh says—we don't wash the dishes to get the dishes clean," he said. "We wash the dishes to wash the dishes." That's not actually what Ven. Nhat Hanh said, but it was close enough to get the point across: Instead of rushing to complete our tasks, we should use that opportunity to practice mindfulness.

My turn to wash dishes came Sunday after dinner. There was a big tub full of dishwater into which my dishwashing partner was loading dirty dishes. I reached into the water for a plate to wash, and I came up with a handful of spaghetti noodles. We'd had spaghetti a few meals earlier, so obviously that dishwater was pretty well used by that point. I told my partner I was going to go get fresh water.

"Oh, but we're conserving water," she said. I understood that, but I didn't think we could get the dishes clean with water that dirty. "Well, remember what Thich Nhat Hanh says," she replied. "We don't wash the dishes to get them clean—we wash the dishes to wash the dishes."

I was groping for a way to politely explain that Ven. Nhat Hanh didn't mean for us to leave the dishes dirty when, to my relief, the pastor came over and told us to get fresh dishwater.

During that retreat, I spent about 30 hours meditating, had one-on-one meetings with the roshi and listened to dharma talks. However, the teaching I got from that exchange about the dishwater stuck with me more than anything else.

A lot of people come to Buddhism wanting to learn special practices like meditation, hoping such practices that will lead to spiritual realization. When they're told to practice while doing a mundane, day-to-day task, they want to turn that task into a special practice. They're missing the point— your life *is* your spiritual path, and its mundane tasks *are* your spiritual practice.

We often see a spiritual path like the Buddha's Middle Way as a "religious" practice. I will talk later about ways to use some of the Buddha's instructions to guide us in meditation and so on, but the Eightfold Path isn't a guide for practice during retreats and services—it is a guide for living.

In Theravada Buddhism, dharma teachers often talk about the Eightfold Path as a threefold training in *sila*, *samadhi* and *pañña*. Sila refers to moral restraint: right speech, action and livelihood. Samadhi refers to meditation and other ways of training the mind; it includes right effort, mindfulness and concentration. Pañña means wisdom or discernment and includes right view and right resolve.

The three trainings are generally presented in that order—sila, samadhi, and pañña, because you won't have much success developing wisdom if you can't train your mind, and it's hard to train your mind if you're killing, stealing, or otherwise behaving badly toward others. Therefore, you should try practicing moral restraint before you jump into meditation.

However, the three also work together; you can't make much progress on one without working on the others. When you try to consistently practice right action, for example, you'll have to bring wisdom to the process of determining what actions are skillful and what actions are harmful, and you'll have to use right concentration and mindfulness to set your mind on your objective and monitor how well your actions reflect your intentions.

For instance, imagine you visit a temple to go for refuge and take the Five Precepts. In that process, you vow to refrain from harmful speech. You go to work the next day determined to keep your vows—you're engaging the samadhi part of the triple training by setting your mind on your vows.

While you're in the office, a co-worker starts gossiping about another co-worker, and you have the habitual urge to join in the gossip. You notice this urge arising—that noticing comes from mindfulness. Because you have listened to and analyzed some dharma teachings, you have acquired the wisdom to realize gossip is harmful speech. With effort, you restrain your mind and refrain from gossiping.

Sometimes I'll hear someone say they want to try practicing the Eightfold Path one "fold" at a time. While it can be a good idea to focus your effort on areas where you have a weakness, you can't ignore the rest of the path. It's like traveling on an eight-lane highway—you can keep your car in one lane, but you still have to travel the whole road if you want to get from one end to the other.

It makes sense when you approach these three trainings as a practice to begin with the moral restraint of sila and then move to meditation and finally wisdom. However, we're going to approach the three trainings in the order in which they appear on the Noble Eightfold Path. I think they're more accessible as teachings that way, which is perhaps why the Buddha presented them in this order when gave his first sermon to set the Wheel of Dharma in motion.

To follow this spiritual path is to loosen the ties that keep us in the cycle of stress and suffering. By coming to terms with the truth of life, setting our minds on compassionate action, and training our minds, we can cultivate the antidotes to dukkha: wisdom, compassion and serenity.

WISDOM

The first two factors of the Eightfold Path, Right View and Right Resolve, make up the "wisdom" or pañña portion of the three trainings. As you will recall, to practice Right View means to understand and realize the true nature of life. To practice Right Resolve means to direct our deepest aspirations toward charity, non-violence and selfless concern for others.

You might think of Right View in terms of a belief system—not a system of blind faith, but a way of organizing our views so they help us see more clearly the world in which we live—so we can discern what actions and emotions will lead to less suffering and more peace for ourselves and others.

Right Resolve, then, concerns the volitional thoughts that stem from our Right Views and which lead to actions and emotions—the karma of body, speech and mind—that lead away from suffering and toward peace and happiness.

There are several core teachings we should consider as we cultivate wisdom. They are often referred to as the Four Seals of the Dharma:

1. **Dukkha.** All compounded things—that is, all things that arise from causes and conditions—are unsatisfactory.

2. **Impermanence** (Pali, *anicca*). All compounded things—all things that arise due to causes and conditions—are impermanent and thus subject to change.

3. **Not-self.** (Pali, *anatta*) All compounded things are not self.

4. **Nirvana** (Pali, *nibbana*) Nirvana is peace.

The First Seal: Dukkha

Dukkha is the first of the Four Seals of the Dharma. In essence, the teaching boils down to this: Stress, suffering and dissatisfaction are a part of life. Disappointments and adversities are a normal part of human existence. Birth, death, aging, illness, being separated from loved ones and associating with that which we dislike—all those things happen to all of us. Rather than battling them, we can view them as steps toward enlightenment.

The Buddha taught that much of our suffering is a consequence of our mental activity. That doesn't mean our suffering is "all in our mind"—it can definitely be in our bodies and behaviors, and it can be affected by the world we live in. However, if we want to transcend dukkha, we need to stop the mental activities involved in its arising.

The Buddha specifically attributed dukkha to processes that are largely cognitive in nature and that fall under the general heading of "ignorance." There's a doctrine that is among the Buddha's main teachings, Dependent Origination, in which the Buddha spelled out the way ignorance leads to suffering.

Dependent Origination is a sometimes confusing concept that works on a number of levels and is often used to explain how the "stains" left by ignorance on our consciousness lead to rebirth. For now, however, I'm going to focus mainly on the humanistic understanding of dependent origination.

The Twelve Factors of Dependent Origination, as the concept is presented in its traditional Pali form, appears like this:

Avijjā-paccayā saṅkhārā,
> With ignorance as a condition there are sankharas (mental formations).

Saṅkhāra-paccayā viññāṇaṃ,
> With sankharas as a condition there is consciousness.

Viññāṇa-paccayā nāma-rūpaṃ,
> With consciousness as a condition there is mind-and-body (nama-rupa).

Nāma-rūpa-paccayā saḷāyatanaṃ,
> With mind-and-body as a condition there are the six senses.

Saḷāyatana-paccayā phasso,
> With the six senses as a condition there is contact.

Phassa-paccayā vedanā,
> With contact as a condition there is feeling.

Vedanā-paccayā taṇhā,
  With feeling as a condition there is craving.

Taṇhā-paccayā upādānaṃ,
  With craving as a condition there is clinging.

Upādāna-paccayā bhavo,
  With clinging as a condition there is becoming.

Bhava-paccayā jāti,
  With becoming as a condition there is birth.

Jāti-paccayā jara-maraṇaṃ soka-parideva-dukkha-domanassupāyāsā sambhavanti.
  With birth as a condition, there is dukkha: aging, death, sorrow, lamentation, pain, distress, and despair.

I've illustrated this with a diagram:

The 12 Factors of Dependent Origination

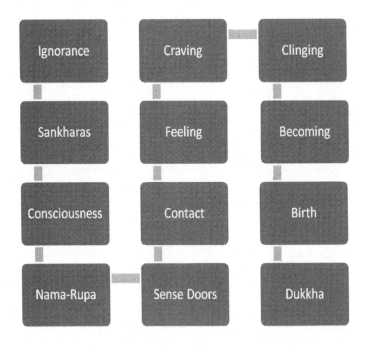

This may seem overly complicated and you might wonder how it applies to day-to-day life. However, dependent origination demonstrates how our experience of events comes equipped with baggage, including ignorance/delusion/irrationality, and thus how our reactions to those events are colored by that ignorance.

Things, events and circumstances come into our awareness through Contact, which is what happens when formless (Nama, or "name only") and form (Rupa) states encounter one another. For instance, you might be sitting on your meditation cushion and develop an ache, which is a Feeling. That ache arises because of Contact, which arises via the Sense Door of touch.

By contact, I don't mean your body's contact with the cushion—it's contact between your mind and your physical form that is of concern here. That contact happens through the senses, which is where mind becomes aware of form.

The Sense Door is only there because Nama-Rupa is there, and that includes Consciousness. Consciousness comes equipped with Sankharas, which are mental processes. Some of those processes are rooted in Ignorance.

Thus the Feeling, which is unpleasant, becomes an object of Craving (I *can't stand* this discomfort, perhaps), and thus a Clinging (I *need* to move). That leads to Becoming—becoming fidgety, maybe, or becoming doubtful that you can get any good out of this practice that's so intolerably uncomfortable.

Thus you experience Birth (in this moment) as a person who gives up on meditation rather than working harder developing concentration and mindfulness, and so you experience the Dukkha that you were hoping to transcend by learning to meditate.

I'll share with you a process I have used in Rational Buddhism sessions to explain this in a little more detail. Rational Buddhism (RB) is not a reinvention of Buddhism. It's simply a tool we can use to help examine the interplay between our cognitions, our emotions and our actions. RB uses principles developed by psychologist Albert Ellis, Ph.D., who pioneered cognitive therapy with Rational-Emotive Behavior Therapy (REBT) in the 1950s.

In RB, we analyze our cognitions and their effects in a very user-friendly, straightforward A-B-C process, with A being a perceived *Adversity* we experience through contact, B being the *Beliefs* (sankharas) we bring to the situation, and C being the *Consequences* (feeling, craving, clinging, becoming, etc.) that arise.

Here's an example: When I'm walking my dog, I'll sometimes encounter a fellow who walks his three dogs in some of the parks I visit. He never has his dogs leashed, and they have attacked mine a few times, although fortunately with no injuries. When I tell him he is supposed to have his dogs leashed, he tells me to stop telling him what to do.

So, at (A), I have a run-in with the dog owner—that's an adversity with which I have contact. At (C), I experience anger and other emotional consequences, which are forms of craving. Because of clinging and becoming, I also demonstrate behavioral consequences, like yelling at the other dog owner (becoming and birth).

If you asked why I was angry, I might say it's because the guy doesn't leash his dogs—that (A) somehow causes (C). However, my anger and the other consequences are not caused by (A) as much as by the beliefs (B) I carry into that experience with me.

Those beliefs include rational beliefs that responsible pet owners obey leash laws and that it's unsafe and inconsiderate not to do so. If I stuck with those rational beliefs, I wouldn't be "okay" with this dog owner walking his pets off the leash. I might point out patiently but firmly that he's breaking the law and creating a nuisance for which he could be fined and which could result in serious injury for his or someone else's dogs, to other people and possibly to himself.

Notice these beliefs probably wouldn't lead to a lack of emotion or to warm and fuzzy feelings, but to appropriately unpleasant emotions like annoyance and concern. Future encounters might lead to disappointment that the dog owner didn't heed my advice.

However, there are also ignorance-based sankharas/irrational beliefs. In the Avijja Sutta, the Buddha defined ignorance as "the leader in the attainment of unskillful qualities." We might predict, then, that these irrational beliefs will not skillfully get me what I want but will unskillfully create hindrances to my happiness, my peace of mind, and my spiritual progress.

My irrational beliefs might include the belief this guy *must* or *should* be a responsible pet owner—that he *should not* put the freedom of his dogs above the safety of others. I also irrationally believe that because he doesn't follow that rule and thus creates a problem for me he's an arrogant bastard—which he *should not* be—and that because I'm personally inconvenienced by his behavior, he deserves an ass-kicking. And when it happens again, I believe he *must not* be so dismissive of my well-intentioned advice and that pet owners like him *should* be easier to educate.

With those beliefs in operation, I might get consequences like anger, low frustration tolerance, and maybe even a violent outburst—all over something that was over in less than a minute and with no actual harm done.

If I wanted to have a peaceful, quiet walk with my dogs and instead got an argument and a lot of obsessive angry thoughts, then what is that? That's dukkha, right? So my ignorance has led, through a series of steps, to my "rebirth" as one who experiences, as the sutra says, "sorrow, lamentation, pain, distress and despair."

However, what was so ignorant about my ideas—so "wrong" about my views that they led to suffering?

First, there's the idea there's a "self" that can be rated—and thus either esteemed or damned—according to some subjective, often very narrow criteria. There's also the corollary idea that others "should" conform to our expectations and if they don't, they're "bad" or otherwise damnable. Finally, we believe environmental circumstances and conditions should support our own goals.

So I might take a look at my view, "Other dog owners *must* act perfectly responsibly; if one does not do as I believe he must do, he is a rotten person that deserves ill will, especially if he stupidly ignores my suggestion to behave differently."

If I examine that carefully with the eye of the dharma, I will see that, while it certainly is *better* if dog owners act responsibly, that doesn't mean they *must* do so. Understanding karma can help us with this one: We all live and act supported by our karma; some of us have the karmic foundation for that level of responsibility, and some of us do not.

While I can talk until I'm blue in the face about how much better it would be if dog owners acted responsibly, any given individual dog owner will act according to his own set of causes and conditions. Yes, it might be stupid for him to ignore leash laws. Yes, it might be unsafe, and so on. But until his own karma brings him to that realization, he's probably not going to do any differently than he already does.

If I look with compassion at the dog owner, I will see the fallacy in the second part of the belief. The other dog owner's actions are the result of delusion and irrational thinking—like mine! I might even recall times I acted less than responsibly and even repeated the same mistake over and over. I don't think that proves I'm totally rotten, so it wouldn't apply to another pet owner.

If I reflect on the effects of this view, I can see how clinging to it could easily lead to more anger. I might even really lose my temper one day and punch the guy, which could land me in jail or earn me a lawsuit. If I can abandon my *self*-oriented insistence the guy *should* act a certain way, I'll at least spend less time angry. With patience and restraint, I might even be able to get the guy to leash his dogs. If not, I can still better enjoy my time outdoors with my own pets.

The teaching on dependent origination doesn't end with just explaining how ignorance leads to suffering, however—as you have just seen, it also explains how to end suffering. If you break any link in that chain of causation, dukkha will not arise. Of course, I could walk my dogs elsewhere so I don't bump into the other dog owner, thus cutting off the process before the point of contact. Or I might be able to let the anger go when it arises so the other effects won't follow.

Many people approach Buddhism as some sort of mystical, transcendental practice designed to get us to some heavenly realm. But when we start practicing, we soon learn that Buddhist experience isn't as much transcendental as it is grounding.

Yes, your Buddhist practice will hopefully help you transcend much of your suffering. However, you'll do that not by reaching some heavenly state so much as by learning how to experience "heaven" in day to day life by confronting and abandoning those thoughts that lead to trouble for ourselves and others—even when that means just dealing more skillfully with other dog owners.

The Second Seal: Impermanence

Since your spiritual life is your day-to-day life, perhaps a good goal for your practice might be to become more aware of your true nature and your relationship to the world you live in. When we look at the world through the lens of Buddhist dharma, we start to see it more clearly; when we see it more clearly, we cause ourselves less suffering. Sometimes that means becoming aware of and cultivating acceptance for life's unpleasant realities.

Impermanence is the second of the Four Seals of the Dharma. Nothing stays the same from one moment to the next—not our bodies, not other people, not conditions and not things. That nice new car is going to get dinged eventually. That hot guy is going to get fat and bald. The new job will become boring, and so on. So if we're attaching our happiness and peace of mind to externals like cars, careers and relationships, we're always going to end up stressed and disappointed.

We expect our lives and our surroundings to be stable, but they just won't live up to that expectation. Since things change over time, when we're attaching our happiness to them—to accomplishments, to other people, to objects and conditions—the happiness will fade as the externals change. We tend to avoid thinking about this, but avoiding reality doesn't protect us from it—to accept it is to transcend it.

There's a well known story about a woman named Kisa Gotami, who lost her sanity after the death of her child. She was carrying the infant's body around her village, appealing to everyone she saw for help, and someone suggested she visit the Buddha, who happened to be staying nearby.

If anyone could help her, a fully enlightened Buddha would surely be the one, she thought. So Kisa Gotami arrived at the Buddha's door with the body of her infant. "My child is sick!" she cried. "Can you please give me a cure?"

The Buddha saw the child was long past helping and realized Kisa Gotami had gone mad with grief. However, he told her he could make some medicine to cure her child. She would only need to bring him a few tiny mustard seeds, and he would make the medicine. Mustard seeds were a staple of Indian cooking, so finding a few of them would be no problem. Practically dancing with joy, the distraught mother started to run away to fetch the spice.

"Wait, there's one thing," the Buddha said. "The seeds must come from a house that has never known death."

Kisa Gotami ran to the first house she could reach and asked for the seeds. The family had mustard seeds, of course, but they were mourning a deceased relative at that very moment. She ran to the next house, and then the next, and so on through the village. At house after house, someone had died or someone known to the family had passed away. There didn't seem to be a single household in the village that had never known death.

As the reality of impermanence sank in, Kisa Gotami's sanity began to return and her overwhelming grief was replaced by wisdom and a feeling of peace. She handed her child over for cremation and returned to thank the Buddha for bringing her back to sanity.

Did she stop missing her child? Did she stop feeling the loss? No, probably not. However, she stopped losing her mind over her loss. Her extreme distress was because of her ignorance of impermanence. Once she understood and accepted the reality of impermanence and of dukkha in this visceral, in-the-gut way, she was able to transcend that suffering. Ultimately, she ordained and became an arahant.

The Third Seal: Not-Self

You may sometimes hear that Buddhists say there's no self. That's not quite accurate: The Buddha actually said that what we think of as a "self" really isn't a discreet, enduring self but an ever-changing process that is inextricably connected to all other things.

While meditating, the Buddha examined form and saw that it was not self—the Pali term is *anatta*. He looked at feelings and saw they were not self; at perceptions, mental formations and consciousness, and all those things were not self.

Our self is a compound thing that arises due to causes and conditions, like all other compounded things. Each self's causes and conditions are dependent on other causes and conditions—these causes and conditions are all related. Thus the idea of not-self also includes the concept of Interdependency.

Earlier, I mentioned the analogy of a wave on the ocean, which ties in with this concept. To a surfer riding a particular wave, the wave seems like a separate, discreet thing. However, the wave really is made up of matter and energy. You can't remove the matter from the other causes and conditions and still have a wave.

What we think of as a "self" is much like that. We think of it as something discreet with a beginning, middle and end. We also think of it as "mine," as if we had some control over it. However, a self is really a wave-like flow of form and mind, constantly changing and related to everything else much like the wave is related to the ocean.

The principle of anatta means there's no intrinsic, inherent self that stands alone, discreet and apart from causes and conditions. The Buddha explained that what we think of as a self is actually a compound made up of five constantly changing aggregates (Pali, *skandhas*).

The first of these aggregates is form, which is made of physical elements—things that come from the earth, from the air and from water, along with "fire," the energy that is released as form changes, which is what animates our physical body.

Then there are the formless aggregates. There are *feelings*: things that feel pleasant, things that feel unpleasant, and things that feel neither pleasant nor unpleasant. There are *perceptions*, which is what happens when the mind comes in contact with form. So as you read this, for example, your eyes, which are form, come in contact with the light that travels from the page to you; your eyes and nervous system communicate about that to your awareness, so that's the perception of images.

Your *conditioned mental formations* then identify that image and start judging whether it's good, bad, boring, interesting or whatever. And then your *consciousness* is aware of all those things happening.

Those aggregates are constantly changing, and we have little control over that change. We can influence it, but not control it. So I think, "This is my body." But the body isn't mine. If it were mine, it would be a lot better looking and less creaky. It's just an ever-changing process subject to causes and conditions. One of those causes and conditions is karma—the results of my willful actions—but that's only one of many such conditions.

At the Zen retreat where I got the "washing dishes teaching," the roshi gave me a koan to work on. Koans are little stories with problems to solve. They're not meant to be solved logically, but more directly experienced. The koan she gave me is called "Joshu's Mu."

Mu is a Chinese character that's the opposite of "is." It's sort of like "is not," but more like "not-is."

Joshu was a famous Chinese master. One day, a troubled monk approached him to ask for guidance. As they were talking, a dog walked by. Seeing the animal, the monk asked, "Does that dog have Buddha nature?"

Joshu shouted: "Mu!"

The master wasn't saying the dog didn't have Buddha nature. Of course dogs have Buddha nature; the whole premise of Mahayana Buddhism, including Zen, is that all beings are headed for liberation, and that's possible because all beings have Buddha nature. Buddha nature is *true* nature—*your* true nature, *my* true nature, *the dog's* true nature.

The problem in the koan isn't about whether or not the dog has Buddha nature—it's about why Joshu shouted Mu. There's no one right answer; to solve the problem requires you to let go of the idea that questions and answers about our spiritual lives need to make sense to the intellect.

When you encounter tough teachings, don't fret a lot over trying to make sense of them. Instead, try to figure out how you'd put it into practice. To me, this is what Mu is about: In order to really enter a spiritual path, you have to transcend some of the dry intellectualization and start living the life.

That doesn't mean we need to submit to blind faith or anything like that—we can keep our healthy skepticism and still continue to learn intellectually. At the same time, however, we find that wisdom and knowledge are not interchangeable, and we stop relying so much on knowledge and start trusting our wisdom more. Rather than staying attached to ideas about Buddha nature, we let go of those concepts and experience our own Buddha nature, which means we embrace the teaching with our heart, not our head.

I mention all this because there are a couple of other related terms—*emptiness* and *oneness*—that I will discuss here. These concepts are difficult to fully grasp intellectually. They're better understood gradually, with practice, from the heart.

You could say the five aggregates that make up a self are all empty of self. Form, feelings, perceptions, fabrications and consciousness are not "mine," because they're subject to change, to causes and conditions that are outside and apart from anything resembling a "self." Once you realize that, you have taken a step toward realizing oneness, the interdependency of all causes and conditions.

Not only am "I" empty of a self, but *all compounded things* are expressions of emptiness. Consider the book you hold in your hands right now, for example. You look at it today and see a book, but there are a lot of non-book things that had to be in place before this book could be here: trees, obviously, and the trees need water and sunshine, so those are in there, too. And there was a writer and editor, a printer, trucks and truck drivers, and so on. All kinds of people and things, living and inanimate, had to be in place before you could hold this book.

But this book also requires *you*, doesn't it? To be what this book "is" to you requires your perception of it and the mental formations that go along with that. You might see it as a good book and a source of wisdom. Someone else might see a boring book, someone might see a confusing book and someone might even see an evil book. For this book to "be" as we think of it existing, that "be"-ing also requires the mind that perceives it.

I used another term here, *interdependence*. In essence, interdependence means that for one thing to be, something else has to also be. For example, you couldn't remove the tree from the book, or the sun, the rain, the author, generation after generation of dharma teachers, and so on. If you removed any of those things, the book wouldn't be there.

There are a number of scriptures where a monk realizes: "When this is, that is. When this ends, that ends," and is suddenly enlightened by this realization. If we realize the fallacy of self, we'll stop clinging to it. And if we realize the fallacy of "other" through the realization of interdependency and oneness, we can transcend some of the stress we have about relationships.

When we look carefully at what we think of as self, we realize there's no separation between my self and the other. You can't just understand that intellectually, however. You have to learn to live it.

One way we practice that is through *gassho*. Gassho is a Japanese word that refers to the gesture of putting your hands together in front of your heart. (It's called *anjali* in India.) It's considered a form of respect, but it can also be a gesture representing oneness. One palm symbolizes the subject and the other palm is the object, and they come together into one gassho.

You might gassho to the Buddha, your parent, your teacher, spouse, or whomever. It not only represents gratitude and respect to them, but oneness with them. Through gassho, the dualism, this artificial separation we impose with names and labels is transcended into naturalness, the true nature of oneness.

So when I gassho to the Buddha, I'm becoming one with the Buddha. If I gassho to you, I become one with you. By the way, you don't gassho with your hands. Your hands make an outward gesture, but the true gassho is done with your heart.

The Fourth Seal: Nirvana is Peace

Many people think of nirvana as a place or a state that is to be attained or reached, perhaps through rebirth after some more enlightened future lifetime. Different traditions and different teachers within traditions are going to define nirvana differently, and I will discuss touch on some of those, but I will stick with a mainly humanistic view of nirvana.

Nirvana is often described as being beyond words—indescribable. When I encounter one of these "beyond conceptualization" ideas in Buddhism, I try to see it in terms of the question, "How do I practice this?" You might think the statement "Nirvana is peace" isn't an instruction for practice, but what if you make it one? I think we can see this seal like this: There is a way to *practice* peace, and as a result, to practice nirvana.

In many cases, that's going to mean letting go of something that seems to have a payoff—your anger, for example, your "need" for approval or your insistence that life be dukkha-free. In the process, you come to understand letting go of it brings about a more peaceful life, a more peaceful mind.

Life is what you make it. And as you're looking at life in terms of oneness, you may really start to see things differently and get a totally different view. The more you cultivate awareness of reality and the fact that we're really supported by the world we live in, the better life looks.

There's another important concept that fits in here, and that's the law of karma. Karma means "action," and we're mainly concerned with willful actions and their results. I talked earlier about causes and conditions. There's a phrase that applies to the cycles of birth, suffering and death—"conditioned existence." By what are these things conditioned? By karma—by action.

There's a long-running dialogue in philosophy about nature and nurture: Are people born good or evil? Are they made good or evil? Do they have a choice to become good or evil?

In Buddhism, the answer is "all of the above." Each of us is heir to our karma. We arise due to causes and conditions. Some of those causes and conditions include actions from our past lives, which we might interpret as social and genetic preconditioning. We're all born with some amount of hard-wiring in place in terms of our mental abilities and personality tendencies, and we're born into families and societies that encourage certain behaviors and discourage others.

In a sense, it is both our nature and our nurture that makes us what we are. But then there's another factor, which is our present karma—our current willful actions. Yesterday morning, you might have said, "Oh, well, I guess I'm just fated to be an angry person," or an anxious person, etc. That belief would have been partially justifiable, because you didn't know any better and you were subject to all that preconditioning.

Today you know better. You've studied the dharma, so now you know the law of karma: If you do a good thing, you get a good result; if you do a bad thing, you get a bad result. In other words, if you keep at it—keep training your mind and restraining your body—you can change the kind of person you are.

You can, in effect, purify your karma. You're not stuck with it. You can accept yourself as a being whose karma put you into this realm populated by mistake-making, flawed humans who have to struggle with greed, anger and delusion. However, you can also recognize that working with these human self-defeating thoughts and behaviors that arise in response to adversities actually brings you closer to liberation from them.

If you decide you want to become a Buddhist, there will probably be some sort of Ti Sarana service offered, during which you formally go for refuge in the Buddha, Dharma and Sangha and take the Five Precepts.

Think for a moment about what it means to go for refuge. You're going for refuge from your own suffering—from the ways you've been creating suffering for yourself—and you're hoping for peace. Sometimes, people become Buddhists hoping for enlightenment, a state that will appear or in which one will arrive after achieving a certain level of realization and which will take one to the ultimate peace of nirvana or a heavenly realm upon death.

Recall that the term nirvana means "unbinding." When one eliminates the impurities that serve as fuel for suffering, the consciousness no longer clings to it. In Theravada Buddhism, one is considered enlightened only after becoming an arahant, one of the Noble Ones who have eliminated all the mental formations that cause clinging and thus have so thoroughly purified their consciousness that it no longer seeks physical form. Thus the cycle of birth and rebirth comes to an end.

Mahayana Buddhists perceive this somewhat differently. Rather than seeking to become arahants and thus escaping birth and death, they stress becoming a Bodhisattva, an enlightened Buddha-to-be that accepts rebirth in order to help others also become enlightened.

In either case, Nirvana cannot successfully be sought for a selfish purpose. The Bodhisattva ideal helps prevent Mahayana Buddhists from clinging to the hope of imminent liberation. Theravada Buddhists know selfish people don't become arahants, so they share the good results of their practice by dedicating merit after they give offerings or train their minds through chanting, meditation or listening to dharma talks.

In either case, when we go for refuge in the Buddha, the Dharma and the Sangha, we are recognizing that there is a better way of living, and we vow to adopt that better way of life.

We go for refuge in the Buddha not because he's a divine being who can "save" us, but because he was a human being just like us who attained a perfect, true peace by doing things we can do. We go for refuge in the Dharma because the teachings explain how to walk that path. We go for refuge in the Sangha because those monks and nuns carried the teachings down from the Buddha's time to today, but also because they serve as examples that others can reach liberation by following the Buddha's path.

You could say you don't go for refuge so you can *reach* nirvana, but the refuge *is* nirvana. Rather than seeking happiness in that which leads to suffering, you seek happiness in enlightened living. Rather than hunting peace, live peacefully—and living peacefully is nirvana.

COMPASSION

The second of the three trainings, *sila* or moral restraint, involves practicing compassionate conduct in the form of Right Speech, Right Action and Right Livelihood. Compassionate living involves two things—refraining from actions that cause harm and performing acts that are helpful.

For example, to practice Right Speech means to speak truthfully, kindly, and courteously to all. That includes refraining from wrong speech. The Buddha listed four forms of wrong speech: lying; using words that provoke anger and discord; abusive speech; and idle chatter.

However, the other side of the equation involves doing things that are helpful. The Buddha pointed out some beneficial ways of speaking, such as speaking with sincerity, friendliness and kindness.

Right Action means behaving in a way that is peaceful, benevolent, and does no harm to others. To practice Right Livelihood is to earn one's living in such a way as to avoid harmful consequences

Some of this was covered in the sections on Dana and Sila in the chapter on Gradual Instruction, where I discussed the importance of cultivating a giving mind and following the behavioral guidelines of the five precepts. There are a couple of other important factors to consider and some related topics we will explore in this section.

In the last chapter, we looked at karma as it relates to the idea of a self and to self-acceptance. Karma also plays an important role in the cultivation and expression of compassion. Just as understanding the role karma played in putting you where you are and making you what you are, you can also take into account that others are the heirs to their own karma.

If we truly understand the effects of karma on the people around us, we tend to act more from compassion and less from anger and greed. Even if we don't like the way others act at times, we can accept them as fellow suffering beings, too.

I touched briefly in the previous chapter on the idea of purifying one's karma, and compassion plays an important role in that. When you think about purifying your karma, recall first that karma means action, specifically willful action. We normally think of action as something with physical expression that could be seen externally. However, the Buddha talked about karma in terms of actions of body, speech and mind. When training in compassion, you will need to be mindful of all three.

Remember the law of karma: When you do a good thing, you get a good result; when you do a bad thing, you get a bad result. The good you do— mentally, verbally or physically—dilutes and washes away bad results. The more good you put out there, the more the bad results are diluted. This sounds like some sort of magical, mystical thinking, but it's pretty practical, really.

Imagine, for example, a teenager who begins abusing intoxicants and eventually steals to support his habit. These are bad actions, obviously, but as long as the adolescent gets away with these things, he continues to do them. The more he does them, the more his mind is tainted by the bad actions and the more he becomes "criminal" in his thinking. Even though he has not been caught and punished, having that criminal mindset is the bad result of doing the bad things.

What if he goes to prison, however, and, like many of the Buddhist inmates I meet, he begins to hear about the benefits of training the mind to not cling to every craving that comes along? At first, meditation and hearing dharma talks have little effect. The more he listens, meditates, and practices compassion toward others, however, the more he wants to change his life for the better. In time, he overcomes at least some of the effects of his bad actions by accumulating the effects of good actions.

As we have seen, the physical training in compassion also involves training the mind. And the opposite, cultivating compassion as a mental state—which is an action of mind—supports training one's actions of body and speech.

Some meditation practices, such as the Tibetan practiced of Tonglen, are specifically intended to help cultivate compassion. Tonglen means "sending and receiving," and the practice involves bringing different people to mind. As each arises in the mind's eye, the meditator imagines some of their suffering and symbolically breathes it in; breathing out, the practitioner imagines sending them whatever antidote they need.

If there's someone you know who is angry or depressed, for example, you imagine yourself accepting that anger or depression as if you're relieving them of it, and then you breathe through it and send them friendship or joy. The purpose isn't some ritual that is supposed to alleviate suffering; rather, the point is to develop the ability to recognize and accept suffering and react to it with compassion.

I learned about this practice some years ago while I was working with meditation to resolve some personal anger issues. I realized its effectiveness one day while my wife and I were running errands. We were harried and rushed, and we hadn't eaten, so we stopped at a fast-food chicken place. Behind the counter stood a middle-aged man who was, to put it mildly, somewhat brusque.

He watched impatiently as I looked at the menu overhead. "I'd like a two-piece, spicy, white meat with fries," I said.

The man behind the counter leaned back and glared at me as if I had just said the most offensively stupid thing he could imagine.

"You want a number three!" he growled. "How can you expect me to get your order right if you order it like *that*?"

My blood began to run hot—I could feel the flush starting up my neck. But then a strange thing happened. Instead of laying into him, I saw the guy's suffering—his aching feet, his frustration, his loneliness, his fatigue—rising off him like black smoke. I allowed myself to breathe it in and imagined sending out the opposite of all that as a radiant clear light.

I smiled and said, "Sure, okay, I'll have a number three."

I thought my wife was going to faint. We got our order, and she was silent as we walked to the car. "You started doing Tonglen, didn't you?" she said.

Buddhists are sometimes criticized because of our apparent emphasis on inner peace. People look at a Buddhist monk meditating in the forest and staying apart from the world and ask, "Isn't that being selfish?"

It may seem really self-serving to sit there cultivating inner peace and transcending your own suffering while there's all this injustice and war and hunger in the world. However, you'll be a more effective agent of change if you know how to restrain your mind, and you'll create less misery for yourself and others, too. Also, cultivating internal compassion has a tendency to take form in external compassion, too.

A relatively new movement called Engaged Buddhism seeks to become a formal outward expression of compassion. I was once asked to speak at a church on Engaged Buddhism, and the woman who invited me wondered, "What does it mean to 'be engaged?' Is it about engaging with your life? With the people and problems in your life? Engaging with your spirituality? Or something else entirely?

I thought that was a really interesting question. As you have already seen, nothing in the Eightfold Path stands alone; part of its beauty is that everything works together. Engaged Buddhism usually refers specifically to Buddhist activism, but it can mean all those other things, too. I think it's best to approach it first in light of engaging with the mind, and then to consider how to use that awareness to connect your life and your spirituality.

I mentioned the Buddha had a son, Rahula, who was born shortly before he set out to seek enlightenment. When he was seven, Rahula ordained and became a monk. One day not long afterward, the Buddha asked him, "Rahula, what is a mirror for?"

Rahula said, "For reflection."

The Buddha then explained the value of reflection: "When you're doing something, or speaking, or thinking, stop and consider—This thing I'm doing, saying or thinking, does it cause me any harm? Does it harm someone else? And if so, stop doing it."

So when you start practicing compassion, you have to first understand what's harmful and what's not, and you have to resolve to do what's helpful and not harmful. Second, you need mindfulness—you need to train your mind to reflect on what you're doing. Finally, you need effort to get yourself on track and keep yourself there.

The Tibetan teacher Lama Thubten Yeshe told a story about a man who decided he wanted to get more serious about his Buddhist practice. So he went to a stupa, which is a shrine that houses holy relics, and he began walking in circles around it. Purifying one's karma by circumambulating sacred structures is a customary practice in some Asian countries.

As the man is walking in circles around this stupa, an old monk happens by. He watches for a moment and then says, "You know, circumambulating the stupa is fine, but maybe you should practice the dharma."

So the man thinks about this and says, "Well, this old monk probably means I should be studying the scriptures." So he starts going to the temple and studying the scriptures. Again, the monk happens by one day, and he says, "Studying the scriptures is fine, but maybe you should practice the dharma."

The man is frustrated now, so he asks around: What could this old monk mean?

Someone says the monk meditates a lot—maybe he should try that. So the man starts going to the meditation hall to sit. One day he opens his eyes and sees the monk looking at him. "Meditation is fine," he says. "But maybe you should practice the dharma."

So now he's really frustrated. "Practice the dharma! Practice the dharma you say! What do you mean by practice the dharma?"

In this particular story, the old monk explains that for the guy to make spiritual progress, he needed to stop his ego's clinging to the attitudes that are keeping him stuck in samsara. But I think the real point of this story is that "the dharma"—and that includes your own spiritual practice—doesn't mean doing something special. It means being aware of your life as you're in the process of living it.

Thus we could say having an engaged spirituality begins by using mindfulness to stay present with our life, moment by moment. Tonglen, for instance, is a meditation practice, but you don't do it so you'll get good at meditating. You do it so that, when you encounter someone's suffering, you'll recognize it as such and react with compassion. You engage with your mind by becoming aware of what's going on in the mind. You then use that awareness to engage with the world, whether that's in church or on a meditation retreat or in line at a fast food restaurant.

In Bright Dawn, we practice the Way of Oneness. We acknowledge our oneness with all beings—our sense of community with all life. I think this way of looking at things is very much in line with the concept of interdependency that is reflected in the practice of Engaged Buddhism.

Recognizing the web of interdependency isn't just a cool thing to do: It also means becoming aware of our responsibility for those with whom we share that web, which includes all life. In Buddhism, with our emphasis on the importance of compassion, we come to understand karma not just as something that will lead to a better life for the individual, but we also recognize what professor of Buddhist art and culture Ronald Y. Nakasone called a "karma of universal goodwill that labors unceasingly to lead all beings to spiritual ease." (Nakasone)

Once you begin to see yourself as an instrument of that "karma of universal goodwill," a natural extension could be to let your compassion manifest as social action. The Buddha was kind of a social activist himself, and he encouraged followers to practice both for their own benefit and the benefit of others. He also pointed out that to protect oneself by developing virtue is to protect others. In the Anguttara Nikaya, for example, the Buddha sets out the ethical standards, and he explains non-harming as an act of generosity:

> *In refraining from doing harm, one gives freedom from danger, from animosity and from oppression to limitless numbers of beings. In giving this gift, one gains a share in limitless freedom from danger, from animosity and from oppression.*

Engaged Buddhism, then, could include conscientiously choosing day-to-day actions that give ourselves and others freedom from danger and oppression. If there is oppression, we can try with our speech, actions and livelihood to not help the oppressor grow stronger. And where we can, we help right the wrong.

The concept of Engaged Buddhism originated with Vietnamese monk Thich Nhat Hanh. During the Vietnam War, monks had to face the question of whether to stay in the monasteries meditating or to go help those who were suffering from the bombings and other effects of the war. Ven. Nhat Hanh decided to do both.

It wasn't enough just to understand and have compassion, he said. That's part of it, but we should remain aware that the world is suffering, people are hungry, and social injustice is occurring—and then act with love and compassion. Otherwise, we're not practicing Buddhism; we're just escaping.

However, he said we should start by looking deeply into the situation, first peering into our own hearts and the hearts of those who may treat us unjustly so that we understand the causes and conditions that underlie the oppressor's actions. If we can find the causes that underlie social injustice, we won't condemn the person. And, he adds, a dualistic response, one motivated by anger, will only make matters worse. (Nhat Hanh)

Ajahn Mun, a Thai forest monk who became an arahant, was once asked for a "victory protection" of some kind. When he considered the request, the verse arose in his mind: "Conquer anger with non-anger."

That is the most important dharma to practice, he said. Anger can destroy a society. But as long as living beings have love and kindness in their hearts, there's a chance the desire for happiness will be fulfilled. Without love and kindness, even with all the material comforts in the world, our lives will be devoid of genuine peace and happiness.

If you want to practice Engaged Buddhism, I suggest developing Ajahn Mun's victory protection at every opportunity. Learn to conquer anger with non-anger and to conquer oppression with non-oppression. Of course, we're only human, and it is a complicated world. It's not always easy to see the most compassionate choice. But we can always look into our heart and let it guide us.

You may also look at your livelihood as a spiritual practice. To practice Right Livelihood means to earn one's living in such a way as to avoid harmful consequences. Many people broaden the idea of livelihood to include one's lifestyle.

When the Buddha spoke in specific terms about livelihood, he mentioned refraining from activities like selling poison or weapons. However, he also asked householders to live without exploiting others, cheating or otherwise harming their customers and colleagues. We might also consider the importance of living without harming our communities.

Ideally, we should develop a livelihood that not only includes how we earn our living, but balances that with other important activities like spending time with family, getting adequate exercise, eating well, and getting adequate rest.

In ancient Japan, some of the old Zen masters would walk up to a monk and shout, "Show me your Buddhism!" If the monk didn't give the right response, the master might whack them with a stick. So what would you do in that situation? Fall down and start meditating? Run to the altar and do prostrations?

Usually, after getting whacked a few times, a monk would figure out, "Oh, what I'm doing now! That's my Buddhism!" Raking leaves, wiping down the woodwork in the living room, answering the phone, waiting on a customer—that's your Buddhism, so you should be fully present with it in this moment.

It's easy to see your vocation as a spiritual path if your job is to be a monk who can meditate and do spiritual duties most of the day. It can be much harder when you have a house, mortgage and job.

However, besides spending six years in ascetic practices, Gautama was trained in the kinds of knowledge a leader would need. As a prince whose father had wanted him to be a great king, Siddhartha got the education he needed to become a good leader.

After he was enlightened, the Buddha not only spent a lot of time teaching monks how to practice, but he advised some of his era's great kings and business leaders. For example, his biggest lay supporter was a businessman named Anathapindika, who formed a trade organization to export goods from India to other regions. The Buddha taught a comprehensive spiritual program, and he meant for people who have to go to work every day to be able to realize the fruits of spiritual practice, too.

Although Right Livelihood falls in the second section of the threefold training where the focus is on compassionate action, remember that nothing in the Eightfold Path stands alone. In one of the early scriptures, the Buddha explains how Right Livelihood fits in: Right View is "the forerunner," he says, because one needs that wisdom to discern whether a livelihood is right or not. Then one uses Right Effort to abandon wrong livelihood and enter into a right livelihood and uses Right Mindfulness to see, on a day-to-day basis, whether the livelihood stays "right" or not.

Mostly, the Buddha leaves it up to us to figure out what sort of occupation is Right Livelihood. Generally, you should be able to do your job without "breaking training"—without breaking the vows you made when you took the five precepts.

The Buddha does give a few concrete suggestions about wrong livelihood, though: we shouldn't make our living by trading in weapons, slaves, intoxicants or poison, or raise animals for slaughter. However, you have to use your judgment about statements like that. A doctor prescribes an antibiotic, for example, which is poison to bacteria. However, the doctor isn't trading in dead bacteria—the antibiotic is protection for his patients.

There are a couple of stories that give us a pretty good idea what sort of things the Buddha wants us to consider mindfully as we earn our living. In one, he talks to an actor, a man named Talaputa, who's the head of a troupe of actors. Talaputa comes to the Buddha, respectfully sits to one side, and asks, "According to the ancient teaching lineage of actors, 'When an actor on the stage makes people laugh and gives them delight, then after death he is reborn in the company of the laughing devas.' What do you say about that?"

The Buddha says, "Don't ask me that."

Undeterred, Talaputa asks again, and then again. Finally, the Buddha says, "Okay, since you keep asking, I guess I'll have to answer you." He then explains that if an actor sets his mind on inflaming the passions, anger and delusions of people who are already impassioned, angry and deluded, he'll be reborn in the hell of laughter.[5]

He has a similar exchange with the leader of an army who believes warriors who die in battle will be reborn in a special heaven. Again the Buddha tries not to answer, but finally explains that if one goes into battle preparing to harm others, there's a hell for that, too.

Even if you don't buy into the idea of rebirth in a heaven or hell, these stories still make a good point. The Buddha didn't dislike performers or military people, but consider what he says about livelihood and its relationship to views and mindfulness: If you are intent upon causing harm or unmindful about the harm you're causing, that's not going to have a good effect on your own mind—and heavens and hells are created in the mind.

If doing your job involves killing people or trading on people's tendency to deride others, to have revenge fantasies and so on, doing your job will have harmful karmic consequences. You're going to harm others, but you're also doing damage to your own mind—you're compromising your wisdom, your ability to be compassionate, and ultimately your serenity.

In the middle-length sayings, the Buddha gives us some more thoughts on what constitutes wrong ways to make a living, telling us we shouldn't have to use "trickery, cajolery, deceit, or dissembling," to make money. Also, our job should not be characterized by "rapacity for gain upon gain." In other words, one's livelihood should have more to it than just making more and more money for its own sake.

However, the Buddha did encourage laypersons to build wealth. In India in those days, there were people whose main purpose was to seek spiritual liberation and share their knowledge, and their livelihood depended on the generosity of those who sought their counsel. So if everyone who became a Buddhist renounced the world and became a monk, it would be pretty hard for monks to survive.

However, the Buddha pointed out we should use our wealth mindfully. He said to be careful to not lose our money through neglect and inattention, but he also laid out some guidelines for where to apply our wealth. One scripture outlines a whole hierarchy of ways to use one's wealth, beginning with taking care of yourself, your spouse and children, and then helping out friends, relatives, the needy, and your spiritual support network.

The Buddha was very progressive in his advice to employers. They

---

[5] Talaputa Sutta

should assign chores according to each worker's ability, he said, and they should pay their employees adequately, give them promotions and bonuses when they earned them and take care of their health care.

I'm sure life was difficult in ways we can't imagine during the Buddha's era. In many ways, however, our lives are more complicated today. With our technology, our lifestyles and livelihoods are so interconnected that we really have to be careful what we do if we want to avoid harming our fellow beings, our environment and even ourselves.

The Buddha told monks and laypersons alike to cultivate the Brahma-Viharas using methods like Tonglen. In the next two chapters, I'll discuss that and other ways to cultivate kindness, joy and equanimity. One way to make your workplace into your spiritual path is to cultivate these states of mind and then try to practice them while you're at work.

It will be hard, but it's worth the effort. Can you imagine how nice the workplace would be if everyone practiced kindness toward one another, tried to help each other avoid mishaps, genuinely took pleasure in one another's successes and managed to keep their cool when things didn't go well?

SERENITY

Imagine standing alongside a pool of water—dirty, muddy, muddled water, its surface stirred by a strong wind. No matter how good your eyesight nor how intently you peer into the water, whatever lies deep within is hidden from view so long as the pool remains stained and sullied by sediment and its surface clouded by ripples.

Now imagine the pool becoming serene: The wind dies down and the surface becomes calm; the mud begins to settle and the sediment accumulates on the floor of the pool; the water slowly clears. Now, without straining, almost effortlessly, you can see fish darting between the stones and shells that lie on the bottom.

Most of the time, our mind is like that muddy pool, constantly clouded by the chaos of thoughts, of judgments, of do-lists, of rehashes of the past and anxieties about the future. Just as the wind keeps the surface of the pond agitated, the constant assault of external sights and sounds agitate our senses; and just as the sediment darkens the water itself, so our anger, attachments and misunderstandings darken our awareness.

As long as our minds remain clouded, we are unable to view the wisdom that lies deep within. With training, however, we can let the mind grow serene. That's where the third of the three trainings, samadhi, comes in.

These last three factors on the Eightfold Path—Right Effort, Right Mindfulness and Right Concentration—refer specifically to training the mind. Bright Dawn explains Right Effort as the practice of striving diligently to overcome anger, greed, and ignorance; Right Mindfulness means to remember and cherish the qualities of wisdom and compassion; and Right Concentration involves setting one's mind on fully on becoming one with the reality of life in all its forms in the eternal now.

Practicing Right Effort, Right Mindfulness and Right Concentration may include meditation, although it is important to remember that it is not necessary to meditate to practice Buddhism, and training the mind is an ongoing process that doesn't begin and end at the door to the meditation hall.

There are different practices for training the mind that don't involve sitting quietly doing nothing. For example, many people find the Japanese practice of Naikan, which involves keeping a gratitude journal, to be very helpful.

However, I encourage you to try meditation, and current research shows there are significant physical and mental benefits to be gained from its practice. Meditation has been credited with helping people manage pain and to quit smoking and recover from other addictions. It may enhance sleep, lower stress and help reduce anger, anxiety and depression.

Several studies published in the last few years have demonstrated that meditation derived from Buddhist practices helps increase attention span and cognitive functioning. In one such study, groups of 30 people attended a meditation retreat led by Buddhist scholar B. Alan Wallace while another 30 acted as a control group. Participants took part in several experiments, and the results showed that practicing meditation improved visual perception and attention span.

In another study, psychologists found that a group of 49 participants practicing meditation for 20 minutes per day showed a significant improvement in their critical cognitive skills after only four days. A third study of 27 people who actively practiced different styles of Buddhist meditation showed they have stronger connections between brain regions and show less age-related brain atrophy than non-meditators.

Researcher Fadel Zeidan, a post-doctoral researcher at Wake Forest University School of Medicine, worked on a study in which meditators focused on the breath in a relaxed manner while being mindful of mental processes that arise. In the report he co-authored, he compared meditation to exercise—"like working out a bicep, but you are doing it to your brain."

Only a few decades ago, there were relatively few resources in America for people who wanted to learn meditation. Today, we have almost the opposite problem: There's so much information it's hard to find a solid starting point, and you can quickly get confused by the countless practices and forms of meditation.

When you boil it down to the basics, however, Buddhist meditation is not really all that complicated. Meditation deals in three main areas: concentration (Pali, *samadhi*); mindfulness (*sati*); and *bhavana* or cultivation of particular mental states. Different practices tend to focus more on one or the other, but all three work together.

In any case, there is typically a meditation object—the "thing" on which you rest the awareness. There are probably an infinite number of possible meditation objects, but the breath is a good place to start. Breath is always with you and it doesn't have any particular spiritual or religious significance. Also, once you begin concentrating on your breath, you'll find it gives you a lot of useful information about how your body and mind interrelate.

It's good to start by practicing concentration, because concentration leads to calmness or tranquility (*samatha*). Think about that muddy pond. Letting the mind settle on an object is like letting the water settle in the pool. As long as the water stays agitated, it remains cloudy; if the water is allowed to be still long enough, even the finest speck of dust will settle to the bottom. As you rest your mind on the rise and fall of the breath, all that "dirt" clouding your mind will settle down. Your mind will gradually become calmer, and thus clearer.

Mindfulness means being fully aware and fully in the present. If you're concentrating on your breath, for example, and anger arises, you're aware of the anger. However, you don't go chasing after it—if you perpetuate the anger, that means you're not in this moment and in this place. Perhaps you're in some other moment and place in the past when the anger-related event occurred or in the future when you get to tell off the guy on the cushion next to yours because his growling stomach is "distracting you."

Practicing mindfulness leads to insight (*vipassana*). There are different insights available to you when you meditate. For example, if you're practicing mindfulness, you notice that you feel angry about the rumbling stomach next to you. You then notice that the guy's stomach isn't really distracting you at all—your mind went off to explore this rumbling stomach instead of staying with your breath.

Right Effort is involved here. When mindfulness alerts you to the presence of anger, you use effort to abandon the anger and to cultivate its antidote, compassion. Rather than perpetuating your anger, you examine the elements that make it up—the mental fabrications, the physical sensations that arise from it, and so on. In the process, you may learn you've built a big chunk of your "self" around the idea that other people should control their stomach grumblings so you can have a peaceful meditation retreat.

If you look at this closely and mindfully, you can see the three main Buddhist teachings in this one event: anicca (impermanence—of the stomach rumbles and of your fleeting meditative tranquility); anatta (not-self, as in the "self" you were going to protect against this distraction); and dukkha (unsatisfactoriness of impermanent, insubstantial existence.)

The third factor in meditation, *bhavana* or cultivation, incorporates both concentration and mindfulness but uses contemplation to actively develop certain states of mind, especially *metta, karuna, mudita* and *upekkha*. The Buddha called these mental states the Brahma-Viharas, which means the Divine Abodes, because they represented the highest, most transcendent mental states.

Metta is often translated as "goodwill" or "lovingkindness." It refers to the desire for a sentient being's happiness and welfare. The Buddha didn't often tell us to believe something in particular, but he did ask that we accept and acknowledge that all beings want to be happy and to avoid suffering, so metta is your heartfelt belief that their happiness is good. To cultivate metta, you begin by acknowledging your own desire for happiness and then extend that desire for happiness to include others.

You could say metta falls under the heading of Right View—understanding happiness. Thus karuna—compassion—falls into the category of Right Intention. You want others to be happy and free from suffering, so you resolve to help them when you can. You cultivate karuna by generating a strong desire for others to be free from suffering and then you cultivate the willingness and ability to accept their suffering and return it with kindness.

Because you want others to be happy and to avoid suffering, you will take joy in their good fortune. That joy is mudita. You may see this translated as "sympathetic joy," but I think you could also consider it universal gratitude. You can cultivate gratitude, the realization of your interconnectedness to the world and the joy that arises from that realization, and then expand that gratitude to include others.

Finally, despite your good wishes and good intentions, you know bad things will happen to yourself and others. That's where upekkha comes in. Upekkha, which is usually translated as "equanimity," is the ability to not get upset when things don't go as we'd like. As Albert Ellis would put it, you refuse to make yourself miserable; Reinhold Niebuhr would say you have the serenity to accept that which you can't change.

While unskillful states of mind like anger and anxiety lead to stress for ourselves and others, the Brahma-Viharas lead to reduced stress and increased happiness. With mindfulness meditation, if you notice you have anger, for example, you might see how it causes you trouble and learn you can let go of it. However, if you also cultivate its "antidotes," metta and karuna, you loosen anger's connection to you while you increase your capacity for love and caring.

The next chapter contains instructions for cultivating the Brahma-Viharas and for other meditations. However, there are a few more things you should have in mind before you start trying to meditate.

First, remember that the purpose of meditation is to train the mind. The Buddha sometimes talked about the "monkey mind" jumping from one distraction to another. If you've ever had to leash-train a puppy, you know what that's like. You pull the puppy over, make it sit, and it immediately jumps up and runs to play. So you pull it over again, make it sit, and it runs off again. You do that again…and again…and again…and finally the puppy learns what "sit" means. The mind in meditation can be a lot like that puppy.

Whenever your mind strays from the meditation object, just patiently, compassionately bring it back. If you're meditating on the breath, don't try to push thoughts away or force them not to arise. Simply let it go and return to the breath…let it go and return to the breath…let it go and return to the breath.

People often expect meditation to be a peaceful, enjoyable experience, and they're disappointed when they spend the allotted time struggling. It is nice when the mind settles down and becomes calm and when we get up from our meditation cushion feeling refreshed and relaxed. However, those relaxing meditations aren't necessarily the "best" ones—sometimes we get much more from a half-hour of struggling.

Also, people sometimes have interesting or profound experiences during meditation one day and then want or expect the same thing to happen the next. Don't go into your meditation session with any particular expectation. It's much better to go to the cushion determined to train your mind, and then take whatever happens as a teaching.

As you begin to meditate, remember that a successful practice will include Right Effort, Right Mindfulness and Right Concentration.

Right Effort is a two-part process. First, with mindfulness be aware when harmful mental states arise. Then when they arise, use effort to abandon them and to prevent their return. Second, be aware whether or not helpful mental states are present; if they are not, cultivate them and maintain them.

Harmful mental states fall into three main categories—the "three poisons" of greed, anger and ignorance. As you meditate—and as you go through your day—you can use mindfulness to watch for the arising of greed, for instance, which includes all forms of clinging and craving, not just the financial form. You use mindfulness to notice when anger arises, and you use mindfulness to be watchful over the arising of ignorance in all its forms, including the irrationality we discussed earlier.

During meditation, we can watch specifically for the Five Hindrances to meditation: sensual desire; ill will; sloth and torpor; restlessness and anxiety; and doubt.

Sensual desire takes a lot of different forms. During meditation retreats, for example, almost everyone at least once experiences a longing for the bell that signals lunch-time. Of course, sensual desire can arise as lust, but it can also arise as an urge to watch television show or listen to music—or even just to move to a more comfortable place to meditate.

Anger will often show up as thoughts over a past injustice. Restlessness may appear as anxiety, worry or an urge to run through your do-list or mentally plan your grocery shopping. Sloth may take the form of depression or ennui, and it may also be the result of fatigue.

Doubt can be very subtle. This isn't doubt in the form of healthy skepticism; rather, you doubt that you have the ability to do the practice, or you feel you're not "getting anywhere" and that the practice itself is somehow not working.

There are different ways to respond when you notice one of these states arising. Generally, however, you want to abandon it. In other words, note it and drop it. Be aware that it's there, and without evaluating it or yourself for having it, just leave it behind—just let it go.

Don't push it away, deny you have it or condemn yourself for having it. You are human, and humans have these tendencies. If you can't easily let go of the thoughts associated with it, then try mindfully and non-judgmentally observing it. If you have anger, see what it feels like in your body. Where is it located? Does it expand and contract? Does it come and go?

You can do the same with desire, with restlessness and with all the others. If there is anxiety, how does it feel? Is it with you forever, or will it eventually pass away? What about fatigue? What does it feel like? Can you brighten your mind and make the fatigue less heavy?

You may also challenge the thoughts associated with these states. What happens to anger, for example, if you look at it in light of not-self or karma? What happens to anxiety if you consider it in light of impermanence?

Notice, by the way, that effort, mindfulness and concentration work together in this process. You may be concentrating on your breath and then notice with nonjudgmental awareness that your attention has drifted away to thoughts of a rude comment a coworker made earlier, and now you feel angry. You use effort to abandon the anger and return to concentration on the breath.

In time, your concentration stabilizes and you enter a jhana state, a refined and focused meditative absorption. With mindfulness and effort, you maintain that carefully balanced concentration.

These are called the Five Hindrances because they prevent us from keeping our minds set on our meditation object. However, these states don't just arise while sitting quietly trying to concentrate—they also arise while we're at work trying to keep apart from the gossip-fest or while we're dealing with a difficult family member and trying to stay calm. They hinder us in countless situations where we struggle to keep our mind focused on our long-term peace and happiness rather than short-term gratification.

If these mental states create trouble during your meditation, they are probably creating trouble in the rest of your life. Meditation and the rest of the Eightfold Path offer you a way to look deeply into the causes behind their arising and ultimately loosen the roots that anchor them in your consciousness.

At the same time, you can cultivate and nurture skillful states like kindness and joyful gratitude. Thus freed from these hindrances and protected by wisdom and compassion, you can begin to savor the serenity that is your natural state.

MEDITATION

I attended a meditation retreat where the teacher insisted that after the retreat ended, everyone should meditate for one hour twice each day. I wonder how many of the people who attended that retreat do that? I suspect most probably tried for a few days but soon gave up.

If you read a dozen books on meditation, you'll find a dozen opinions on when, how often and how long to meditate. Don't worry about meditating for the "right" amount of time or doing the "right" meditation. Everyone is different, and what's right for someone else might not be right for you. Also, you can expect your "right" meditation to change as you progressively realize the fruits of the practice.

Some people start by meditating a few minutes per day and work up from there, while others learn how to meditate by going to retreats where they immediately begin spending most of the day meditating. I suggest trying different things and seeing what works for you.

How much time you spend meditating has to fit in with the reality of your life and lifestyle. It would be pretty pointless to "plan" to meditate for an hour twice a day and then not meditate at all because you didn't have two hours to spend. I believe it's far better to plan to spend five minutes per day and do as you planned!

As in training the body, however, consistency is the key to progress. Most people seem to do better if they can meditate at the same time (or times) each day. Also, stick with whatever you've planned. If you've set aside 20 minutes to meditate on the breath, don't switch to cultivating metta after five minutes and then give up after 10 minutes—then you have let your monkey-mind (or puppy mind) take charge of the training.

The following Harmony and Gratitude meditations are good for beginners. They don't take very long, so you might consider using these to help you establish a habit of meditating regularly and then move on to some of the other practices.

Harmony and Gratitude

Harmony and Gratitude are Gassho practices adapted from teachings by Rev. Koyo Kubose. These simple practices involve short morning and evening meditations—contemplative meditations that use discursive thinking to help cultivate skillful mental states.

These can be integrated into your existing practice by putting them at the beginning or end of a meditation period, or they can be done on their own. While they can certainly be performed at a "sacred space" like an altar or in front of an image of the Buddha, they can be done during any opportunity for a few minutes of inner quiet.

Morning practice: Harmony Gassho

Begin by establishing a comfortable, relaxed posture that will allow you to breathe deeply. Take three "cleansing breaths," inhaling as if you were filling your lungs from the bottom up, expanding your lower diaphragm, upper diaphragm and lower chest, and finally upper chest, even allowing your shoulders to rise toward your ears if you like. Let your shoulders relax as you exhale from the top down, continuing to exhale until you've pushed all the air out of your lungs.

As you breathe out, first let go of any physical tension, then any mental activity, then any emotional tension.

Let your breath find its own rhythm. Rest your awareness on the breath, silently letting the word "harmony" ride on your exhalations for a few moments.

Think of two or three ways you could develop more harmony in your life and your surroundings today. Try to be as specific as you can, and consider any opportunities to develop the three virtues: your wisdom, compassion and serenity. In other words, what can you do to see disharmony as a result of your own ignorance and craving; how can your behavior be more helpful and less harmful to others; and what hindrance can you try to let go today?

Try to formulate these as simple statements (like "be nicer to Bob" or "let go of my 'need' to be 'right'") and repeat them to yourself a few times.

Finally, to complete the practice, put your hands together in gassho and breathe deeply three times, each time mentally reciting the word "Harmony" on the out-breath.

Evening practice: Gratitude Gassho

Repeat steps 1-3 as above, but this time let the word "gratitude" ride on the breath.

Think of two or three things for which you are grateful. This may seem difficult if you're experiencing tough times—if you're in prison or separated from a loved one, for instance. But even in the midst of difficulty there are good things for which you can be grateful—a helpful mentor in your life, a good cup of coffee, a friend, a cool breeze or a bird's song.

Try to make at least one of these an opportunity to develop mudita—appreciation for the good fortune of others. If we can only feel grateful when our own desires are satisfied we have far fewer chances for joy than if we include the happiness of others in our reasons for gratitude.

Again, try to restate each simply and repeat it to yourself a few times.

Put your hand together in gassho and breathe deeply three times, each time mentally reciting the word "Gratitude" on the out-breath.

~ ~ ~

Anapanasati (Mindfulness of Breathing)

Meditation on the breath is probably the most universal form of meditation, and virtually every Buddhist meditation tradition teaches some variation of it. Anapanasati—mindfulness of breathing—is the first form of meditation mentioned in the Satipatthana sutra, where the Buddha lays out the path to mental purification through the foundations of mindfulness.

I learned this way to meditate on the breath from my teacher in the Thai tradition. I encourage you to learn it following all seven steps, but with practice you will probably find you settle into concentration before you get to the final stage, and that's fine.

Seven-Step Anapanasati

Find a comfortable posture and turn your awareness to your breath. Take several deep breaths, expanding your diaphragm first and then your chest until your lungs are completely full. Breathe out letting the breath flow out of your chest and then contract your diaphragm to empty your lungs completely.

One: Experiment with breathing different ways. Breathe in long and out long; in long and out short, letting the breathe flow out quickly; in short and out long, letting the breath out slowly. Try short in- and out-breaths. Be aware how the breath feels in your body as you breathe different ways.

Two: Stop controlling your breath—just let it settle into a comfortable rhythm. Rest your mind on the breath, noting each breath with an anchor word or phrase. One traditional anchor is the word "Buddho"—you think silently to yourself as you breathe in, "Bud-"

and as you breathe out, "Dho." If you prefer, you can use "Rising/Falling" or "In/Out."

Three: Explore the path your breath takes as it flows in and out. Rest your awareness on the in-breath for a while, feeling each breath flow in through your nostrils. Shift your awareness lower, feeling each breath pass across the area at the back of your mouth where the sinuses empty toward your throat. Move your attention to the base of your throat; to your lungs; to your diaphragm. Feel your diaphragm rising and contracting.

Four: Explore the path the breath takes leaving the body, feeling the air flow outward past each of those points. Feel your lungs emptying, the air passing up through your throat, past your palate, out your nostrils.

Five: Explore your body with your breath. Stay with your breath, but let your awareness scan your entire body. Start with the toes—rest your awareness there and notice any sensations as your breath flows in and out. Continue this up your foot, moving from point to point up your body, feeling each part of your body with your breath until you reach the top of your head.

Six: Now rest your awareness at the tip of your nose or your belly, wherever you feel the breath most distinctly. Just stay with your breath there.

Seven: Keep refining the breath, calming it, until the mind is still. Sit with open awareness until the breath and mind become one.

When preparing to leave meditation, take your time. You may want to sway gently to feel yourself in your body before you open your eyes. Rub your hands together to warm them, if you like, and press them gently over your face and eyes. Finally, bring your hands together in gassho to symbolize oneness.

~ ~ ~

Cultivating Goodwill

I mentioned the Brahma-Viharas in the last chapter. Many people find cultivating those mind states to be a very effective use of one's meditation time. The Buddha often recommended it as a practice useful not just to monks but to people from all walks of life, and I have found it personally to be very powerful. Meditating on the breath or other mindfulness-based meditations may be, over the long term, your most useful "core" meditation practice, but it is worth taking the time to explore the Brahma-Viharas.

Cultivating the Brahma-Viharas begins with metta. In this meditation, you begin by wanting happiness for yourself, and then go from there to wishing happiness for a loved one, a good friend, a neutral person, someone hostile—someone with whom you have some conflict—and finally all beings.

With this practice, we first establish the idea that happiness is good. We acknowledge that it's a goal we have and that it's a good goal. We also acknowledge that the goal is attainable. If we don't have happiness now, we can work toward it.

That's an important idea: Happiness comes from working for happiness. It doesn't just happen to us or fall on us from the sky. It's attainable through our own efforts. So when we think, "May I be happy," we're thinking, "May I do the things that cause happiness and abandon the things I've been doing that get in its way."

It's hard to care for others when we're busy creating suffering for ourselves. If I'm creating suffering for myself, I'm probably visiting that on others in one way or another. Also, we see that happiness grows when it is shared.

We next wish for happiness for others, just as we wished for happiness for ourselves. We don't need to define what that means or should mean for them, but as we go along, we try to break down the barriers between our desire for happiness for ourselves, our loved ones, friends, and even people we don't like.

You should expect to encounter some resistance, but keep working on it. Notice the origin of your resistance, how it feels, and how the feeling changes when you begin to let it go.

Metta-Bhavana

Sit comfortably and spend a few moments just quietly observing the breath. Begin cultivating metta by opening to yourself, directing the sense of loving care, friendship, kindness and connection to yourself. Spend a few moments contemplating the good that lies within you, and acknowledge your desire for happiness.

Direct metta to yourself. There are a few traditional phrases: May I be happy; may I be free from animosity; may I be free from stress and affliction. Use those or choose others that reflect your desire for true happiness. Let the phrases emerge from your heart and "ride" on the breath. Be aware of any feelings that arise in connection with the phrases.

Direct metta to a benefactor. Send this same desire for happiness toward a parent or someone who has cared for you, inspires you, or otherwise reminds you of your capacity to be loving, compassionate and aware. Envision that person or say their name quietly to yourself and imagine she or he is sitting with you.

Offer them the same wish for happiness you wished for yourself: May you be happy; may you be free from animosity, may you be free from stress and affliction.

Expand your metta to a good friend. In the same way, direct metta toward someone you like and whose company you enjoy.

Send metta to a neutral person. Choose an acquaintance, someone you neither like nor dislike. All beings everywhere want to be happy. Even if you don't know this person well at all or understand their karma, you know they, like all beings, want happiness. Wish for them the happiness you wish for yourself.

Send metta to a hostile person. Think of someone difficult and include them in your circle of metta. Be aware of any feelings that arise and view any resistance as an opportunity to expand your ability to cultivate goodwill.

Let your goodwill become boundless. Send metta to all beings everywhere, without distinction: "May all beings be happy. May they free from animosity. May all beings be free from stress and affliction."

Continue sending metta to all beings in all directions. You might send metta to all beings that walk on the earth, fly in the sky, swim in the water, or burrow underground. Or go from your community to your state, your nation, the continent and so on.

~ ~ ~

Cultivating the Brahma-Viharas

After practicing Metta-Bhavana for some time, you will be able to break down the walls between yourself and the people you love, like, are neutral towards and have problems with. At some point, you're going to find it fairly easy to enter into jhana with each of them.

Jhana, which means "meditative absorption" is a refined, focused mental state—as if the mind is "absorbed into" the object of meditation. In this context, it means you use the thought, "May I be happy," or whatever you're cultivating, to generate a *nimitta*—a sensation or other mental phenomenon—that goes along with that. You'll get absorbed into these sensations and thoughts without losing concentration.

Ultimately, we want to start with metta for ourselves, enter into jhana; move to the loved one without losing that jhana; then to the good friend and so on through the hostile person and then all beings, maintaining that absorption the whole time.

Then you move on to compassion and use the same system, sending a desire for freedom from suffering. It may work better for you to start with yourself, or you might get better results beginning with someone you want to help. I find it easier to generate feelings of compassion if I start out with someone I want to help, and then move to the loved one, friend, neutral person, hostile person, and all beings. However, sometimes having compassion for myself comes into play, too, especially if I'm having trouble relating to one of those people.

Go to mudita, this time starting with your friend. Develop gladness for their good fortune, whatever that may be. Get that gladness going and keep it going, saying, "May you enjoy your good fortune" as you move from one person to another. Then take a moment to be thankful in general for the support you receive from all beings.

Finally cultivate equanimity. There is a traditional set of verses that go with that, and you may want to memorize it. Otherwise, come up with a statement for yourself that sums up the idea that we are all owners of our karma, heirs to our karma, and so on. It is best to begin with the neutral person here and then move to the loved one, friend, hostile person and finally all beings, including yourself.

To go through that entire process may take an hour or more. There are ways to shorten that if you don't have an hour to spend: You can contemplate all four Brahma-Viharas but emphasize one of them in depth. You can also go straight to "all beings."

You may also start with Metta-Bhavana and go from there, based on whatever arises. You might be sending metta, for example, and find that someone arouses compassion. Another person might have had some good luck, so share enjoyment of their good fortune.

There's no one "right" way to do this. There are traditional ways, but you can use common sense, good judgment and your own wisdom to be aware of what's going on and make use of whatever arises.

It's always good, though, whatever you do, to finish with equanimity. It's great to cultivate compassion and metta, but it's even better to temper that with the reality-check equanimity requires—you need that reminder that happiness and suffering are compounded things and therefore are impermanent.

It may help you to memorize the following traditional Brahma-Viharas verses and use them as the basis for your cultivation:

Metta

May I be happy.
May I be free from animosity.
May I be free from stress and affliction.
May I live peacefully.

May all beings be happy.
May all beings be free from animosity.
May all beings be free from stress and affliction.
May all beings live peacefully.

Karuna

May all beings be freed from stress and suffering.

Mudita

May all beings enjoy their good fortune.

Upekkha

All beings are the owners of their karma, heirs to their karma.
Born of their karma, they are all related by karma.
All beings live supported by karma.
Whatever actions they do, good or evil, they will inherit the results.

~ ~ ~

Meditating on the Virtues of the Buddha

The title of this book came to me when I had been meditating on the virtues of the Buddha and was trying to come up with a way to formulate that process into something I could pass along to others. This meditation is the result.

Most of the time, we associate Buddhist meditation with practices of mindfulness and concentration that don't involve actively thinking "about" anything. Thoughts arise during Anapanasati, of course, but our response to that is to let them go and return to the breath.

If we're practicing a more spacious-awareness kind of meditation, we're aware of things that arise, we note them, and let them be without judging them. We might also apply a momentary recognition of dukkha, anicca or anatta to such phenomena, thus simply acknowledging their inherent stressful, impermanent or non-self characteristic.

However, sometimes working with more directive thinking, which requires engaging our cognitive processes, can be helpful, and there's no reason not to use that when it seems appropriate. If you're working through a specific problem or learning how to apply the dharma to daily life, contemplating and cultivating the virtues of the Buddha—wisdom, compassion and serenity—can be a very productive adjunct to less directive forms of meditation.

<u>Wisdom ~ Compassion ~ Serenity</u>

Establish awareness on the breath. Begin using the virtues of the Buddha—wisdom, compassion, and serenity—as anchor words to connect the breath and awareness. Continue noting your breaths with "wisdom, compassion, serenity" as you call to mind the situation you wish to investigate with these virtues.

Wisdom

Begin looking at the situation in terms of wisdom—that is, in terms of understanding dukkha and the cause of dukkha and developing intentions that lead to skillful action.

Consider what kinds of suffering are involved: Is this the physical dukkha of aging, illness or mortality? Or is this the dukkha of not having what you want or of getting what you don't want?

Remember the root cause of suffering is ignorance—a lack of understanding, a misunderstanding or an irrationality. See if you can identify the misunderstanding here. Usually, the ignorance manifests as some sort of ego-attachment or ego-aversion.

If the suffering comes with anger, for example, you may be clinging to the idea that there is an "I" that others "should" try to please. If the dukkha comes with restlessness and anxiety, your ego may be clinging to the idea that this "I" should be perfect, or that there is a "self" that is somehow controlling and should be under control.

If the dukkha comes in the form of ennui or depression, the ego may be clinging to the notion that life should be free from dukkha. If the suffering is in the form of craving, the ego may be insisting on external sources for happiness.

Try to see this situation for what it is—see if you can understand the circumstance free from the ego-clinging.

Compassion

Now consider the dukkha as an opportunity to practice compassion. Where does compassion fit here?

Can you see your own "self," compassionately, as a wave on a sea of karma seeking freedom from suffering? Can you compassionately help your ego let go of the causes of dukkha?

Can you see others in this situation in that same light? Without necessarily liking their actions, can you see how their behavior is the result of their karma, and wish them freedom from suffering?

Serenity

Begin thinking of serenity. Consider the nature of a mind freed from the misunderstandings and misguided attitudes you've been using to approach this problem. How would your actions—physical, verbal and mental—be different? How would that feel?

Remember that nirvana isn't something to be "attained" in some future life. It's available right here, if you can let go of these attitudes and let the pure mind emerge from your wisdom and compassion.

~ ~ ~

Whenever you finish meditating, take a moment to dedicate the merit from the practice—to resolve to share the good results that come from your work. This act has several important effects.

First, to share our merit reminds us that we are interdependent with all other beings. Our actions of body, speech and mind do not just affect us, but also everything around us. Thus the good we do affects others, also.

Second, this keeps us from clinging to the results of our practice, because we're not selfishly hoarding the results that will take us to higher spiritual plateaus. To share our blessings also gives us another opportunity to cultivate a giving heart.

I hope you will try these meditations for yourself. Don't get discouraged if your meditations don't always seem to go smoothly. I said this before, but it bears repeating: Meditation is a method of training the mind, and sometimes when you feel like you're struggling and getting nowhere, that's when you get the most benefit from it.

Don't expect too many dramatic flashes of insight. That may happen, but the awakening of insight is often very subtle. Rather than having a sudden epiphany, you may simply realize during the course of your daily life that you view something differently than you did before or you react to stress differently than you had.

It is difficult to learn meditation from a book, so find a teacher if you can. If possible, get involved with a Buddhist community with an active meditation practice, so you can learn from others who have gone through the same things you will experience. If there's not a community near you, perhaps there are retreats you can attend not too far from home.

In any case, good luck and don't get discouraged. Remember that adversities are simply opportunities to practice—to see life clearly through the lens of wisdom, to open to the compassion that blooms naturally in your heart, and to enjoy the fruit of practice as it ripens into serenity.

POSTSCRIPT: THE SPIDER BODHISATTVA

It was around sundown on the fourth day of a 10-day silent meditation retreat. I wanted to go home.

When you tell people you're going on a 10-day meditation retreat, most will say, "Oh, that's going to be so great! It's going to be so peaceful! You'll be so calm!"

I guess if you haven't been on a meditation retreat, you assume that involves spending days sitting in a beautiful, tranquil room with incense and soothing music, exploring deeper and deeper levels of blissful relaxation. The reality is much different. In Buddhism, to meditate is to train the mind. Like any training, it can be hard work.

This particular retreat was a Vipassana course at a center known for strict adherence to discipline, and noble silence was rigidly observed. I didn't mind being silent—in fact, that was the easy part. It was great to have an uninterrupted period for meditation, and it was nice to be able to focus on the activity in my own mind without feeling like there were a dozen other things I should be doing instead.

Except for the last 10 minutes or so of each twice-daily "Sitting of Strong Determination"—Vipassana-speak for "not moving for an hour"—I was enjoying my time in the meditation hall. I didn't even mind that the guy behind me kept snoring.

But I was bored. I missed my wife. I missed my dogs. There were too many arbitrary-seeming rules. The teacher wasn't really very helpful. The recorded chanting, so different from the rhythmic Thai and Japanese chanting I'd done before, crept cruelly up and down my spine like the sound of nails scraping across a chalkboard. Perhaps worst of all, what had over the past few years been occasional bouts of mild tinnitus had grown over the last few days into an incessant drone. It sounded like dozens of cicadas with chainsaws had taken up residence in my skull.

I *really* wanted to go home.

A road ran through the retreat center compound, and we could walk for exercise along a 100-yard stretch of that dirt road and a small trail that led into the Southeast Georgia woods. I had hiked back into the woods and done a little qigong, which was good for my aching knees, and then walked back to sit by the little pond near the meditation hall.

I noticed a spider about an inch long slowly working his way up the stem of a spindly weed. It reached the tip of the plant and then swung off into the breeze, riding a thin strand of silk to another weed. It did this again and again. Strand by strand, the spider patiently constructed an intricate pattern of interlaced silk.

The bell rang, calling us to the meditation hall for the evening "Sitting of Strong Determination." I rose slowly and moved closer to the web. Putting my hands together in gassho and bowing slightly, I whispered a thank you and promised to dedicate the evening's practice to the spider.

My yearning for home had eased up. I was looking forward to the meditation and to being able to dedicate any merit I accrued to the little spider that clung to the web out by the pond.

After breakfast the next morning, I walked over to the pond. The spider was nowhere to be seen, and its web hung limp under the weight of thick dewdrops. By lunchtime, it had completely disappeared. But that evening, I again sat by the pond and watched the spider as, strand-by-strand, it patiently created its marvelous little mandala of sticky silk.

Each day, the web would disintegrate beneath the forces of humidity, sun and wind. Each evening, the spider would rebuild it.

One day, a cold front moved through the South. It rained most of the day; when the storm cleared, a biting, frigid wind blew across the pond. The spider didn't appear that evening. I tried to warm it in my heart as I cultivated metta during the evening practice.

Apparently a night spent huddled and hungry in the weeds is just a natural part of life for a spider—the next evening, it returned to patiently weave its web as if nothing unusual had happened.

The desire to leave the retreat early never went completely away. However, that spider and its web had reminded me that I was not meditating for my own benefit, but for the benefit of spiders and all other beings everywhere. It also gave me a point of focus: My resolve was strengthened by seeing the patient, strong determination the spider manifested as naturally and unselfconsciously as a breeze ripples the surface of a pond.

After loading my car on the final morning, I walked over to the pond. Several days earlier, I had picked up a small stone from my favorite qigong spot in the woods, and I still carried it in my pocket. The sun had not yet arisen, but I could see the ghostly shape of the web faintly outlined with dew in the fading moonlight.

The spider had gone to the weeds for refuge, but I spoke to it anyway. I took the stone from my pocket and set it on the ground as an offering of gratitude. I put my hands together in gassho and bowed, thanking the spider for its teaching.

SOURCES AND RESOURCES

Works Cited

Camus, Albert. *The Myth of Sysyphus: And Other Essays.* New York: Alfred A. Knopf, Inc., 1955.

Nakasone, Ronald. *Ethics of Enlightenment.* Fremont, California: Dharma Cloud Publishers, 1990.

Nhat Hanh, Thich. *Living Buddha, Living Christ.* New York: Riverhead Books, 1995.

Sutras quoted were adapted from a variety of sources. Access to Insight (www.accesstoinsight.org) has a comprehensive library.

Suggested Resources

For more on this book and other books on Buddhism and mindful living, see www.deerparkpublishing.com or email deerparkpublishing@gmail.com:

Bright Dawn Institute for American Buddhism online sangha offers online dharma talks via "Live Dharma Sunday" as well as books and other resources. www.brightdawnsangha.ning.com.

Information about meetings and events, meditation instructions and additional helpful resources are at www.volusiabuddhist.org.

Volusia Buddhist Fellowship
PO Box 893
DeLand, FL 32721-0893

ABOUT THE AUTHOR

Sensei Morris Sekiyo Sullivan first became interested in Buddhism and meditation as a teenager in the 1970s and studied philosophy, religion and psychology in college before receiving his MBA from Rollins College in Winter Park, Florida.

After exploring Zen and some Tibetan practices, he studied meditation and ordained for a monastic retreat at Wat Florida Dhammaram, a Thai Theravada Buddhist monastery. He then took a nonsectarian approach as a dharma teacher and was inducted as a Sensei in the Bright Dawn Center for Oneness Buddhism.

Sensei Sullivan lives in DeLand, Florida. He leads Volusia Buddhist Fellowship meetings, meets with inmates at Tomoka Correctional Institution and speaks regularly at All Souls Unitarian Universalist in Palatka and other Central Florida churches.

Made in the USA
San Bernardino, CA
22 September 2017